THE TEA COUN

GUILD
OF
TEA SHOPS

*The Definitive Guide
to the Best Tea Places in Britain*

1 9 9 6

Published by
The Tea Council Ltd
Sir John Lyon House
5 High Timber Street
London
EC4V 3NJ

Editor: Jane Pettigrew

© The Tea Council Limited 1996
Second edition, reprinted 1995

ISBN 0 9524872 1 7

Design and origination by Roger Simmons Design
Consultancy Limited, The Studio, Entry Hill, Bath BA2 5LY
Printed by Harlequin Colourprint Ltd, Bristol BS4 5QW

CONTENTS

A member of the Tea Council

The Tea Council

Guild of Tea Shops

FOREWORD

Tea cools, calms, refreshes and revives. There is nothing the British enjoy more. Afternoon tea is one of our traditions which visitors to these shores pursue with avid interest. We, ourselves, are equally zealous. Afternoon tea makes a nice break in the middle of a shopping spree; a relaxing and social occasion when taken with friends and family at home, or a treat while out for a walk or a drive.

Within the pages of this Guide, you will find tea rooms and hotel tea lounges throughout the UK. Whilst each place has its own unique qualities, all have one thing in common – a standard of excellence as precisely defined by The Tea Council. All use good quality tea, made and served properly, the food is delicious,

the staff friendly and efficient, the ambience lovely and all offer value for money. For fun and Edwardian splendour, try the tea dance in The Palm Court at London's Waldorf Hotel. All ages are welcome. Or turn the clock back to Victorian times and enjoy tea at The Bridge Tea Rooms in Bradford-on-Avon or at Pasture Farm, Kirton in Nottinghamshire. Perhaps, if you prefer thatched roofs and low beams, then the Strawberry Tree at Milton Ernest or the Thatched Cottage Hotel & Restaurant in Brockenhurst could be your choice for afternoon tea.

Enjoy your tea.

Illtyd Lewis
Executive Director, The Tea Council Ltd

THE GUILD OF TEA SHOPS AND ITS RATIONALE

Apart from tap water, tea continues to be the most popular drink in the UK. Huge sums of money are spent on tea drunk outside the home, in the hundreds of thousands of outlets serving tea in Great Britain.

A recent independent study commissioned by The Tea Council revealed that very few of these outlets conform to the exacting standards of quality that The Tea Council believes desirable.

The Tea Council has therefore concluded that recognition should be given only to those outlets who, in its opinion, meet these very high standards.

This recognition is given by invitation to membership of the unique and prestigious organisation – The Tea Council Guild of Tea Shops.

Only a very few outlets will ever be invited to join the Guild. The hunt for excellence is painstaking and standards are very high. If you come across a gem that you feel deserves to be included, let us know and we will investigate.

Those shops that have been selected are marked on the map on page 9 and you will find further location guides at the beginning of each regional section.

Several of the Guild's member shops operate a no smoking policy and so we have introduced a no smoking symbol 🚭 which you will find on the appropriate pages under the 'Opening Times' for each shop.

TEA SHOPS, TEA ROOMS AND TEA LOUNGES

When The Tea Council first conceived the idea of The Guild of Tea Shops and Guide, its objective was to highlight outlets which used good quality tea, made and served properly to the standards The Tea Council requires for a TOP TEA PLACE OF THE YEAR AWARD nomination.

Nominations for TOP TEA PLACE OF THE YEAR are put forward by the leading food and drink guides and, naturally, include hotel tea lounges as well as tea rooms and tea shops. The tea shop is reputed to have originated in 1864 when the manageress of a London bread shop asked her directors if she could serve and sell tea to her customers when they came in to buy bakery requirements. They agreed and so the tea shop was born.

In the 1830s, the temperance reformers saw tea as the ideal means of combating British alcoholic beverage consumption. They held 'tea meetings' in

Liverpool, Birmingham and Preston, in rooms where tables were laid out with 'tea equipage' and decorated with flowers. Everyone who attended the meetings – some 2,500 people at each gathering – was served tea, and so the tea room came into being.

Tea in the hotel lounge evolved from the custom of taking afternoon tea in the drawing room at home and dates back to the early 1800s, when the Duchess of Bedford decided to sup tea in the afternoon to stave off the hunger pangs that gave her a 'sinking feeling' between lunch and dinner.

The Guild of Tea Shops' Definitive Guide to the best tea places in Britain covers the complete spectrum of tea shops, tea rooms and tea lounges, in cities, towns and country areas. For example, in London you can enjoy tea at the Dorchester Hotel on Park Lane, or in the Oak Room at Le Meridien Piccadilly, or you can cha cha cha at the tea dance in The Palm Court, Le Meridien Waldorf Hotel, Aldwych. Alternatively, try College Farm's Tea House in Finchley – a working farm set in the heart of London, or Le Papillon Patisserie in The Broadway, Muswell Hill. Pasture Farm, in Kirton, Nottinghamshire and The Bridge Tea Rooms in Bradford-on-Avon both have a wonderful Victorian atmosphere, and the five Bettys tea shops in Yorkshire are tea shops in the original sense. For a more modern style try the Pavilion in Eastbourne.

Hotel lounges are not confined to London. In Devon, the Guide recommends Court Barn Country House Hotel, Clawton and The Commodore at Instow; up north, De Vere's Oulton Hall, Leeds, Sharrow Bay Hotel, Ullswater, Cumbria, Bodidiris Hall, Llandeglo, Clwyd by St Tudno, Llandudno, Gwynedd; and in East Anglia, The Swan at Lavenham in Suffolk.

These are just a few examples of the tea shops, tea rooms and tea lounges contained within the pages of this definitive Guide to the best tea places in Britain.

LOCATION OF GUILD TEA SHOPS

TEA HISTORY AND CULTURE

TEA HISTORY AND CULTURE

The early days of tea are wrapped in legend and myth. In about 2737 BC, it is said that the Chinese Emperor, Shen Nung, scholar and herbalist, was sitting one day beneath a tree while his servant boiled some drinking water. A leaf from the tree dropped into the water and Shen Nung decided to try the brew. The tree was a wild tea tree (*Camellia sinensis*).

By the time of the Tang Dynasty (618–906 BC), tea was China's national drink and the modern term 'tea' derives from the early word in different Chinese dialects – Tchai, Cha, Tay – used both to describe the beverage and the leaf. In about 552 AD, Buddhist monks are reputed to have taken tea to Japan. They not only cultivated the tea drinking habit, but also planted seeds and pioneered tea cultivation in Japan. The Buddhists were also responsible for developing the Japanese tea ceremony which is said to be based on Cha Ching (*The Book of Tea*) written by Chinese scholar, Lu Yu, in the 8th century AD.

Until the later part of the 16th and beginning of the 17th century, very few Europeans had heard of tea. The Portuguese and the Dutch were the first traders, transporting regular shipments of the new herb to the ports of France, Holland and the Baltic coast in 1610. Small amounts probably reached England, but there is no record of tea being sold here until 1657 when the merchant, Thomas Garway, offered it in dry and liquid form at his coffee house in Exchange Alley in the City of London. The early coffee houses were favourite meeting places for gentlemen from all walks of life, but ladies drank their tea in the privacy of the home. Samuel Pepys recorded in his diary for 28th June 1667 that he "arrived home and found my wife making a tea, a drink Mr Pelling, the potticary tells her is good for her cold and defluxions."

Through the 17th century, the price of a pound of tea was extremely high, partly because it was still a fairly rare commodity, but mainly because Charles II imposed on it, and other beverages, a very high tax. The high cost led to smuggling, adulteration of the leaves and a thriving black market which did not end until the tax was reduced in 1784.

Gradually, more and more tea was shipped into England and the first tea auction was held in London in the early 1700s. By 1790, Britain had established herself as the centre of the world tea trade.

By the middle of the 18th century, tea had replaced ale and gin as the drink of the masses and had become Britain's most popular beverage. It was taken at almost any time of the day or evening, the upper classes enjoying the habit of serving elegant bowls of tea after evening dinner. At the beginning of the 19th century, the Duchess of Bedford is said to have been the first to serve afternoon tea with some light refreshment and thus started a trend that is still an integral feature of British life.

A PROFILE OF TEA

Tea is an evergreen plant of the Camellia family and is known as Camellia sinensis. It was first discovered 5,000 years ago in China, hence 'sinensis', but in reality, it is indigenous to both China and India. If left to grow wild, tea grows as a tree and can reach a height of some 10 metres. Today, under cultivation, tea is kept to bush size for easy plucking.

Tea varies in characteristic and flavour according to the type of soil, the altitude and the climatic conditions of the area in which it grows. Other contributory factors are the method by which it is processed and, of course, blending together teas from different areas. There are more than 1,500 teas to choose from and they grow in more than 31 countries.

PRODUCTION METHODS

When tea people talk of "making tea", they are not talking of brewing up, but of manufacturing or processing the plucked tea leaves.

There are three types of tea 'make' – green, oolong and black.

Black Tea

Black tea has the largest 'share of throat' worldwide and there are five stages in its making:

(1) *Withering* – the plucked leaf is spread out on trays and left to wither.

(2) *Rolling* or *Cut Tear and Curl* – the withered leaf is broken so that the natural juices or enzymes are released.

■ Orthodox production uses the original type of machine that rolls the leaves to break the veins.

■ CTC (Cut Tear and Curl), or Unorthodox production, uses more modern machines to break up the leaf and release the juices or enzymes.

(3) *Fermentation* – the broken leaf is spread on trays or put in troughs. On contact with air, the leaf juices oxidise (in the tea trade this is known as 'fermentation'). The leaf is turned from time to time until each tray or trough is full of rusty brown broken leaves.

(4) *Drying* (sometimes known as 'firing') – the oxidised or fermented leaf is fed through a warm air chamber

where the moisture is extracted and the tea emerges at the other end where the dark warm brown tea, called black tea, is fed into chests.

(5) *Sorting* – the black tea is fed into a machine with a series of varying sized sieves and outlets. This sorts the 'grades' or different sized leaf particles into chests or sacks before the tea is weighed and made ready for its onward journey to auctions, traders or packers.

Oolong Tea

Oolong tea undergoes the same process as black tea but the fermentation time is halved. For black tea, approximately $3\frac{1}{2}-4\frac{1}{2}$ hours are allowed. For oolong tea this is restricted to $1\frac{1}{2}-2\frac{1}{2}$ hours.

Green Tea

The plucked leaf is allowed to wither. It is then steamed and rolled into a small ball or pellet and dried. The result is a small grey-green pellet of tea.

LEAF GRADES

After processing, black tea is sorted by the size of the leaf particles into different grades. There are two main categories – leaf grade and broken grade. Each grade is sub-divided into further categories. Fannings and 'dust' grades are the smallest particles.

Two tea names which often cause confusion are 'Orange Pekoe' and 'Broken Orange Pekoe'. The names have nothing to do with an orange flavour but denote quality and leaf particle size. Orange Pekoe is a whole leaf grade of tea with plenty of tip and bud which gives the dry black tea an attractive appearance with orange flecks. Broken Orange Pekoe has smaller leaf particles than Orange Pekoe.

SPECIALITY TEAS

Speciality teas are teas that take their name from the area or country in which they are grown; a blend of teas for a particular time of day; a blend of teas named after a person; or a blend of teas to which fruit oils, flower petals or blossoms have been added, thus scenting the tea.

CHINA
Gunpowder

A green tea which, after it has been withered, is steamed and rolled into small pellets without breaking the veins in the tea leaves. These are then dried, and when brewed with boiling water, produce a very light, refreshing and pale-coloured tea. The name is said to have been given to the tea because the pellets look like gunshot or gunpowder of years gone by.

Jasmine

China tea which has been dried with jasmine blossoms placed between the layers of tea. The tea therefore has a light, delicate aroma of jasmine and a flavour to match.

Keemun

A black China tea, bright in colour with a round nutty flavour.

Lapsang Souchong

A large leaf tea distinguished by its smoky aroma and flavour. The story goes that when the Chinese first discovered tea, they used to dry it in the sun. Chinese legend claims that the smoking process was discovered by accident. At some point in China's history, an army camped in a tea factory that was full of drying leaves awaiting processing and so held up the normal working routine. When the soldiers left, the workers needed to prepare the leaves for the market as quickly as possible, so they lit open fires of pine wood to speed up the drying. The tea reached the market on time and a new flavour had been created. Today, the tea is still smoked but by more hygienic, modern methods.

INDIA
Assam

A blend of tea grown in Assam in North India. It is a full-bodied tea with a dark liquor and a rich malty flavour which is ideal as the first cup of tea in the morning. It really wakes you up. Such teas are used in everyday popular blends because of the full-bodied richness.

Darjeeling

Known as the 'Champagne of Teas', Darjeeling is grown several thousands of feet above sea level in the foothills of the Himalayan mountains. Darjeeling teas have a very light delicate flavour.

Nilgiri

The tea from the Nilgiri Hills in Southern India are light, bright and delicate in taste.

SRI LANKA (CEYLON)
Ceylon Blend

Ceylon teas span the entire spectrum of tea production, from low to high grown teas. By blending teas from different areas of the island, Sri Lanka is able to offer a very wide choice of flavour and characteristics. Some blends are full-bodied, others are light and delicate, but all are brisk, full-flavoured and have a bright colour.

Dimbula

Grown 5,000 ft above sea level in Sri Lanka, Dimbula teas are light and bright in colour with a crisp, strong flavour which leaves the mouth feeling fresh and clean. Dimbula was one of the first areas of Sri Lanka to be planted with tea after the demise of the coffee estates in 1870.

Uva

A fine flavoured tea from the eastern slopes of the Central Mountains of Sri Lanka. Uva tea is bright in colour, has a dry crisp taste and makes an ideal mid-morning or after lunch tea.

KENYA

Tea from Kenya is very bright and colourful, which makes it easily distinguishable from its Asian counterparts. It has a reddish, coppery tint with a pleasant, brisk flavour. Kenya tea is widely used in tea bag blends but is ideal drunk alone at any time of the day or night.

INDONESIA

Indonesian Teas are light and flavoursome. Most are sold for blending purposes as this produces good financial rewards in terms of foreign currency for the country. However, in recent years, it has become possible to buy Indonesian tea as a speciality tea. It is extremely refreshing taken without milk, garnished with a slice of lemon, making it an ideal drink for the figure conscious.

SPECIALITY TEA BLENDS

English Breakfast

Traditionally a blend of Assam and Ceylon teas that gives pungency and flavour to help digest a full English breakfast and give a good brisk start to the day. Today, many English Breakfast blends also include an East African tea from Malawi, Tanzania, Zimbabwe or Kenya which gives the blend a coppery brightness.

Afternoon Tea

Traditionally, a blend of delicate Darjeeling tea and high-grown Ceylon tea to produce a refreshing but light tea which makes an ideal companion to cucumber sandwiches, cream pastries and fruit cakes.

Earl Grey

Traditionally, a blend of black China teas treated with the natural oils of the citrus bergamot fruit which gives the blend its perfumed aroma and flavour. Earl Grey tea is said to have originally been blended for the second Earl Grey by a mandarin after Britain had completed a successful diplomatic mission to China.

House Blend

Some menus offer 'a pot of tea', others 'a pot of house blend tea'. This tea is equivalent to – if not better than – the type of tea the majority of us buy to use at home. In tea trade language, it is known as a 'popular brand leading blend'. In catering terms, it will be a Quality Award tea, as identified by The Tea Council's Catering Tea Quality Programme. No matter whether it is loose leaf or in a tea bag, a household tea is a work of art. It can contain 15–35 different teas which are blended in order to consistently achieve the quality, flavour and characteristics consumers expect from their favourite 'popular brand leading blend'. Some of the teas are seasonal, some are not. During the year or plucking season, adverse weather conditions can affect the quality of any of the teas, in which case the blender has to find other teas that will produce the same flavour and characteristics and ensure the consistency and quality of the blend. To do this, a taster/blender will taste between 200 and 1,000 teas a day and will constantly be adjusting the 'recipe' so that we can enjoy our favourite cup of tea all day, everyday, ad infinitum.

Flavoured Teas

Flavoured teas are real tea (*Camellia sinensis*) blended with fruit, spices or herbs. For example, fruit flavoured teas such as apple, lemon, orange, mango or blackcurrant consist of tea blended with pieces of fruit peel or blossom or treated with the natural fruit juice or oil (known as the zest). Spiced tea, such as cinnamon or nutmeg, is tea blended with a particular spice, and herb flavoured teas have the dried herb added to the blend, as in the case of mint or sage tea.

In all cases, the fruit, spice or herb flavours the real tea and should not be confused with herbal or fruit infusions, which contain no tea.

Tisanes and Fruit Infusions

Tisane, according to Roget's Thesaurus, is a soft drink or a tonic. Stemming from the French, the term is used to describe infusions of mainly herbal leaves such as camomile, peppermint, nettle, etc and does not contain real tea. Fruit infusions – today known as fruit teas –

like herbal infusions, do not contain one leaf of real tea. The zest, dried pieces of peel or fruit blossoms, are blended with dried hibiscus leaves to produce a refreshing fruit flavoured infusion.

How to Choose a Good Tea and Store It

When a tea taster, whether a producer, buyer or seller, looks at a tea, there are certain things that he or she can tell by just looking.

For example, the tea must appear 'even'. This means that the dry leaf sample the taster examines is all of the same leaf particle size. Not only does it give the dry leaf a pleasing appearance, but it does mean that when brewed, the flavour and pungency are all released from the leaf simultaneously. An uneven blend – leaf of varying particle sizes – means that when brewing, the flavour and pungency are released according to the varying sizes of leaf particle, giving an unbalanced overall flavour and quality.

Keep your tea in an airtight caddy in a cool dry storage area, away from other strong smelling foods as tea absorbs other flavours very easily.

THE ART OF TEA TASTING

Have you ever watched wine connoisseurs at work? They don't just drink the wine – they hold it up to the light, study its colour and sniff it. Only then do they sip it, rolling it round their mouths with a slurping sound to see if it 'lives up to its nose'. Then they will be able to tell what it is, where it came from and when.

Tea tasters work in the same way. Samples of all the teas being bought and sold in the auctions are tasted and evaluated by the tea brokers and the buyers of the tea that goes into the packets you buy. They look at the colour of the dry leaf, smell the wet leaf and the tea liquor, then they sip or slurp the liquor before spitting it out. Tasters and blenders have some 100 special words to describe what they taste – bright, brisk, full-bodied, etc. In all cases they are looking for quality and flavour and they compare teas with previous growths from individual estates. Tasters working for specific companies are also looking for the qualities and flavour that will keep your favourite blend consistent day in and day out, year after year. No easy task when you consider that tea is a year to year crop, affected by the vagaries of the climatic conditions in the region in which it is grown.

It takes at least five years to train as a taster and most tasters who have spent a lifetime in the tea trade will tell you they are still learning. It is a fascinating art. Like wine, tea is a very personal taste. Experiment with different teas to find your favourite, or you might like to blend your own. A few leaves of Lapsang Souchong or Earl Grey added to your everyday tea will give it a completely new flavour.

What is the best tea? You might as well ask whether champagne is 'better' than burgundy. They are so different, and it depends totally on what you like. But flavour and quality have a lot to do with soil, altitude and climate. The best leaf comes from high altitudes where cooler;

drier air makes the tea bushes grow more slowly, thus producing more 'quality'.

Don't confuse *kinds of tea* (which generally bear the names of the places where they are grown) with *size of leaf*. Leaf size does not necessarily have anything to do with flavour or quality.

Tea tasters use a wide vocabulary to describe the appearance and flavour of tea. The following are the terms used most frequently for the taste of the brewed liquor:

Body: A liquor possessing fullness and strength.

Brassy: Unpleasant, metallic, similar to brass – usually associated with 'unwithered' tea.

Brisk: A 'live' taste in liquor, as opposed to 'flat' or 'soft'.

Burnt: Tea which has been subjected to high temperatures.

Coarse: Describes a harsh, undesirable liquor.

Empty: Describes a liquor lacking fullness – no substance.

Flavour: Very characteristic taste and aroma of fine teas.

Full: A liquor possessing colour, strength and roundness, as opposed to 'empty'.

Lacking: Describes a 'clean' liquor – no pronounced characteristics – lacking body.

Malty: Desirable character in some Assam teas.

Muscatel: Desirable character in Darjeeling teas.

Musty: Suspicion of mould.

Plain: Describes a tea which is innocuous but lacking character.

Pungent: Describes a liquor having 'briskness' – desirable characteristic.

Quality: Desirable attributes of good tea.

Raw: Astringent and bitter-tasting.

Sweaty: Disagreeable taste – poor tea.

Thick: Liquor having substance but not strength.

Thin: Liquor lacking thickness and strength.

Tea – A Digestif

In Britain, we have been drinking tea for more than 300 years. 80% of the nation drink tea daily. We are a nation of tea experts and, although tea shops serve tea, how many times do we hear that restaurants do not?

According to research commissioned by The Tea Council, only 53% of restaurants feature tea on the menu at all, while only 22% of customers request tea when it is not featured.

For a nation of tea drinkers, this is a sad state of affairs, especially when we take into account the history of tea in Britain. Tea has been an integral part of our social and cultural traditions since 1660. Among the middle and upper classes, tea was always served at the end of an evening's social entertainment, both at home and in public places. Working class families also chose tea to accompany their evening meal at the end of the working day. The tradition of afternoon teas was born in the early 1800s and the tea shop in 1884, but neither of these 'new' fashions detracted from the service of tea after dinner.

Throughout its history, tea has always been known for its digestive powers and certainly our forefathers took full advantage of those qualities. So, what caused contemporary Britons to abandon the old traditions?

The root cause can be traced to the aftermath of World War II when many foreigners made Britain their home and many Britons serving abroad were exposed to new social and cultural ideas. The result was a coffee bar boom. Yes, Britain rediscovered coffee. It was what all the young and upwardly mobile drank. More recently, we have seen the fast food and pizza house boom and the popularity of these has nearly eradicated the traditional tea shop from the British scene.

Since its inception in 1965, The Tea Council has done much to redress the balance through catering education and Award programmes which attract maximum media attention, so that the British public are made aware of the availability of good cups of tea out of the home.

Recently, The Tea Council, in conjunction with the Academy of Food and Wine, have developed tea, food and wine tastings which demonstrate conclusively that specific teas enhance the enjoyment of specific foods, wines and liqueurs. For example, Ceylon tea makes an ideal partner for tomato, cucumber or lettuce sandwiches and for rich fruit cakes – a tea time delight. Ceylon tea also pairs very well with lemon flavoured cream desserts and enhances dessert wines or light German style wines.

Kenya tea, with its bright, brisk flavour, pairs deliciously with dark meat sandwiches such as beef or ham. For those who love chocolate cakes and biscuits, Kenya tea is ideal. It also compliments coffee and nut-flavoured desserts, not to mention certain liqueurs such as Malibu, Baileys or Drambuie.

Darjeeling teas go well with English cheeses and cream cheese, cream-based desserts and trifles and cakes such as swiss rolls and Victoria sponges. As a finishing touch to a meal, Darjeeling also partners light dry wines taken with cream cheese and apples.

These few examples demonstrate that tea makes an ideal after-dinner or after-lunch digestif, as well as giving ample choice for a delicious afternoon tea.

If you would like more details of 'Tea Pairing' ideas, please send your name and address with a first class stamp to:

'Tea Pairings' Information
The Tea Council Limited
Sir John Lyon House
5 High Timber Street
London
EC4V 3NJ

TEA AND HEALTH

Tea is a natural product. It contains no artificial colouring, preservatives or flavouring and is virtually calorie free if taken without milk or sugar.

Tea provides an extremely pleasant way of taking in the right amount of fluid that our bodies need daily for optimum health. Tea also contains trace elements and vitamins which help to supplement the body's needs if it is drunk in conjunction with a healthy diet.

Tea is a rich source of two minerals that are essential to health – manganese and potassium. Manganese is needed for bone growth and the body's development. Five or six cups of tea a day will provide 45% of the body's daily requirement. Potassium is vital for maintaining a normal heartbeat and, as one of the major constituents in living cells, it helps to balance sodium, enables nerves and muscles to function and regulates fluid levels within the cells. The same five or six cups of tea drunk daily will provide 25% of the body's needs.

Tea also contains small amounts of the following vitamins: carotene, a precursor to vitamin A, which has antioxidant and protective properties; thiamin (vitamin B1) and riboflavin (vitamin B2) – both essential for releasing energy from food; nicotinic acid and pantothenic acid, which are nutrients linked to the water-soluble vitamins, and ascorbic acid (vitamin C), essential for a healthy immune system.

Tea also contains caffeine. A cup of tea made from loose leaf or tea bag tea contains 40 milligrams of caffeine, and made from instant tea, 30 milligrams. Caffeine is a mild stimulant which can increase concentration and alertness, accuracy and sensitivity of taste and smell. In high doses (more than 800 milligrams, or some 20 cups of tea a day) it can invoke anxiety and unpleasant gastric sensations.

Tea helps us digest our foods and acts as a diuretic. Tea cools, calms, refreshes and relaxes.

THE TEA COUNCIL

The Tea Council is an independent, non-profit making, trade organisation, initiated and funded by the major producing countries and the UK blenders and packers, with the remit to generically promote tea and tea drinking in the UK.

Its activities include:

■ the promotion of tea as a natural and healthy beverage;

■ an Awards Programme for the service of tea in a variety of catering situations;

■ the creation and administration of The Guild of Tea Shops;

■ the Catering Tea Quality Programme, which monitors the quality of catering tea and assures its quality standards, whilst providing a database through which caterers can check the quality of the tea they are using;

■ the Tea Club, for members of the public who love tea and wish to discover more about its taste, history and culture;

■ an industry and trade information service;

■ education tea resources for primary, secondary and further education.

For more details about The Tea Council please write (enclosing name and address and two 1st class stamps) to:

The Tea Council
Sir John Lyon House
5 High Timber Street
London
EC4V 3NJ

THE TEA CLUB

Tea is our most social and sociable drink – a part of our national heritage and daily life for well over 300 years. The Tea Club exists so that its members can share and enjoy the history, traditions and romance associated with this fascinating drink.

Membership costs £12 for membership in the UK, £18 within Europe and £25 anywhere else in the world. When you join you will receive:

■ a letter of welcome;

■ a membership card;

■ a free sample of tea;

■ a copy of the current Tea Club Magazine;

■ the current free gift.

THE MAGAZINE

Mailed direct to you three times a year, in January, May and September, the 16-page Tea Club Magazine is packed with the sort of information tea lovers everywhere will enjoy. It is a bright, entertaining and absorbing publication, featuring in-depth stories about tea, the tea business and its traditions, plus reviews of the latest books on tea and the opportunity to win or buy them at discounted prices.

In March, July and November, a 12-page Newsletter is mailed with lots of special offers, news and general information.

EVENTS

Each year, a number of special events are organised exclusively for members. In the past, these have included anniversary parties at the Cafe Royal and Claridges, a Thé Dansant at the Waldorf Hotel with members of the French Tea Club, a visit to Winslow Hall in Buckinghamshire for a guided tour of the house and gardens followed by afternoon tea with owners, Lord and Lady Tomkins.

EXCLUSIVE TASTINGS

So that you can sample some of the traditional and speciality teas, the club regularly gives members free sachets to taste and compare.

COMPETITIONS

Take a break, make a nice cup of tea and drink it while you puzzle out the answers to anagrams, crosswords and other easy-to-enter competitions.

MEMBER DISCOUNTS

Collectors' Corner in the magazine provides you with tea associated articles at greatly discounted prices. And, as a member, you are also entitled to a 10% discount on any Tea Council mail order offers, such as novelty teapots, mugs, books, infusers or other tea paraphernalia.

For further information about the club or to obtain an application form, please contact:

The Membership Secretary
The Tea Club
PO Box 221, Guildford
Surrey GU1 3YT

TAKE A TEA BREAK

The tea break has been with us for more than 200 years. When people used to start work at the crack of dawn, bosses would give their workforce a cup of tea and a hunk of bread at around 8.30 am.

At the time of the industrial revolution, a group of philanthropists and entrepreneurs did try to ban the 'tea break', maintaining that tea was bad for workers as it made them slothful. However, despite there being no trades unions at that time, the outcry against their attempts was so forceful that the tea break remained in place.

It was also very much part of the rural tradition, especially in the summer months, when flasks of cold tea were carried out to the workers in the fields.

The tea break still remains part of British working lifestyles. Vending machines have tended to replace the tea lady and her trolley; many construction companies are reputed to give their workforce flasks of tea to cut down on time 'wasted' brewing tea; staff restaurants have tended to replace the 'canteen' and tea is often served in single person pots rather than by the cup.

TEA CUSTOMS AROUND THE WORLD

Although the British tend to think of tea and tea drinking as a traditional British custom, tea is drunk throughout the world and the ways of making and taking tea are as diverse as the countries in which the tea is drunk.

In China, it used to be the custom to offer tea to visitors before getting down to the reason for the visit. The tea, usually green and never drunk with milk, was taken in small porcelain cups. This custom continues today.

In India, tea is often made with sugar, honey and spices and sometimes evaporated milk, so that what comes out of the pot is strong and very sweet.

In Bangladesh, tea is boiled in the water and spices and herbs are added to give a hot pungent drink which smells and tastes delicious.

The tea ceremony of Japan is renowned throughout the world but does vary according to region, although the different versions are all based on the same Buddhist philosophy.

In New Zealand and Australia, tea is normally made as it is in Britain, with a great deal of loving care. However, in the outback of Australia, the swagman makes his tea in a billy can. He throws tea into the billyfull of water and boils it up. He continues to let it stew until he is ready to drink it and then keeps the billy hot until it is empty. This can take quite a few hours and the tea gets stronger and stronger throughout the day.

The Australian bushman has a lot in common with the people living in the Middle East who also like to boil their tea in water and then reboil it several times until it is black, bitter and strong.

In some Russian homes, tea is still made in a Samovar, but is more commonly brewed in a pot. The tea is kept warm and poured into glasses with a slice of lemon, or a preserve of some kind, such as strawberry, orange and sometimes honey.

In America, most tea is drunk as iced tea, although the traditional brewing of hot tea is becoming more popular.

Throughout Europe, tea is made very much in the British style, although often boiling water is not used – just hot water – and it is generally drunk without milk and often with an added slice of lemon.

The most important point is that no matter where it is made and drunk, tea is part of a great tradition – widely practised and greatly enjoyed.

Facts about tea

Tea accounts for 42% of everything we drink in Britain, with the exception of tap water. Every man, woman and child (10 years plus) drinks 3.4 cups of tea per day. 70% of the nation drink tea daily. By the time most tea drinkers reach the age of 'three score years and ten', they each will have drunk some 90,000 cups of tea. Approximately 170 million cups slide down British throats every day. It takes four kilograms of plucked leaf to make one kilogram of black tea and the British consume about 150,000 tons of tea per annum.

These are just a few statistical facts about tea, but did you know that:

■ a packet of loose leaf tea – 125 g – will make approximately 55 cups of tea;

■ teabags account for 87% of all tea brewed in Britain;

■ a pack of 80 teabags makes some 125 cups of tea;

■ the tea shop was one of the first steps towards women's emancipation. A tea shop was somewhere an unchaper-oned lady could arrange to meet a friend or friends without sullying her reputation;

■ in the 1700s, a British workman was prepared to spend one third of his weekly wage – approximately 12.5 p – on tea to ensure his family had their daily cuppa;

■ two thirds of the tea drunk in Britain during the 1700s was smuggled into the country;

■ the pantomime character, 'Widow Twanky' in Aladdin, gets her name from the tea trade. The tea ships were known as 'twankys', as were the sailors who manned them. Hence, when sailors lost their lives at sea, their wives became known as Widow Twankys.

■ 'saucering tea' comes from the 1700s when it was considered polite to pour your tea from your cup and sip it from the saucer. In Scotland, when saucering tea, etiquette demanded that you also left your spoon upright in the cup.

A member of the Tea Council

Guild of Tea Shops

The Tea Council

S O U T H   W E S T
R E G I O N A L   M A P

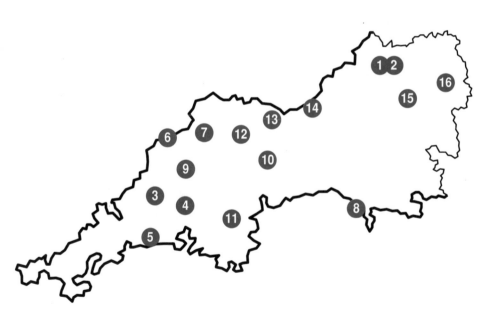

THE BATH SPA HOTEL

Manager: Robin Sheppard

Sydney Road, Bath BA2 6JF
Tel: 01225 444424
Fax: 01225 444006

Directions
From London take the M4 and leave at junction 18. Follow the A4 into Bath city centre. At the first set of lights, turn left following signs for A36. Go over Cleveland Bridge and past the Fire Station. At the mini-roundabout, turn right, then next left after the Holbourne Museum into Sydney Place. The Bath Spa Hotel is 200 yards up the hill on the right hand side.

Opening times
Open all year.

Local Interest:
Just over the river are the Abbey, Roman Baths and Pump Room, Costume Museum and No. 1, Royal Crescent, a Georgian house set in the gracious sweep of the crescent, decorated and furnished in period style. The town is full of interesting little streets and alleyways all packed with shops.

The elegance of the city of Bath is recreated in the sumptuous and traditional English style of the Bath Spa. The original mansion, a Grade I listed Georgian building, was built by a General in the Indian army who was renowned for his hospitality. The hotel continues that tradition today and despite its rather grand period style, is extremely welcoming and has a very friendly, comfortable atmosphere.

Guests have a choice of perfect locations for afternoon tea. They can choose the elegant drawing room (once the library), with its sofas, low tables and bookshelves; the muralled colonnade with its ferns and Lloyd Loom chairs and, in summer, the wonderful gardens where tables are set out under large sunshades.

To draw attention to the importance of afternoon teas, the hotel has an unusual and very clever display of cakes made from dried flowers that sit on cake stands in the drawing room or colonnade. The menu offers a wide selection of equally impressive real food – sandwiches, including toasted and club sandwiches – pastries, biscuits, scones and cakes that are all made in the hotel patisserie. This really is one of the most perfect places to go for afternoon tea. *Teas served:* Darjeeling, Earl Grey, Assam, Lapsang Souchong, Traditional English, Jasmine, Keemun. *Various fruit flavoured teas and herbal infusions are also available.*

THE CANARY RESTAURANT

Owner: Simon Davis

3 Queen Street, Bath
Avon BA1 1HE
Tel: 01225 424846

Opening times
Open all year. Monday–Saturday, 9 am–8 pm
(May–September, 9 am–10 pm).
Sunday, 11 am–6 pm all year.

Awards
1989 Tea Council Top Tea Place of The Year
1988, 89 & 90   Tea Council Award of
                         Excellence
Egon Ronay recommended

Directions
The Canary is right in the heart of Bath, not far from the theatre. The nearest parking is the Charlotte Street car park.

Local Interest:
The Pump Rooms and Roman Baths, the Assembly Rooms and Costume Museum, Royal Crescent and a short walk from Queen Street and all around there are picturesque streets with antiques markets and quality shops.

The Canary is in one of Bath's oldest Georgian cobbled streets, tucked away under Trim Bridge where Jane Austen is said to have purchased her hats. When the parents of the present owner, Simon Davis, bought the restaurant in the 1960s, they kept the name but not the birds that had previously sung in their cages there. Mr and Mrs Davis extended into a second Georgian town house next door and created what is today one of the city's most popular restaurants where afternoon tea is a real speciality and the menu includes copious notes and helpful information about the excellent range of more than 40 high quality teas that are offered.

The downstairs rooms have a comfortable traditional feel, while upstairs, light rattan chairs and tables, lots of plants and a mural of nearby Prior Park create a garden atmosphere. Whichever room you choose, sit back and indulge in a freshly baked bagel or granary bread sandwich filled with smoked trout pâté or succulent roast beef, or a wickedly delicious fresh strawberry tea with clotted cream and wholemeal scones. *Teas served:* 10 House Blends, 5 Darjeeling, 2 Assam, 6 Ceylon, 7 China, Formosa, Oolong, Earl Grey, Jasmine, Pouchkine. *Flavoured teas and herbal infusions are also offered.*

CARPENTER'S KITCHEN

Owners: Debbie and Geoff Beszant

**The Harbour, Boscastle
Cornwall PL35 0ND
Tel: 01840 250 595**

Directions
**Take the B3266 from Camelford or the B3263
from Tintagel. Follow signs to Boscastle Harbour.**

Opening times
Open April–October, 12.30–5.30 pm.
November and March, weekends only.
Open daily during local school half-terms and
Christmas, 10.30 am–5 pm.

Local Interest:
*Walk around this fascinating typically Cornish village
with its narrow lanes and old cottages. Also explore the
site of Bottreaux Castle and 60 acres of the surrounding
National Trust cliffs and land with walks in all
directions and fantastic views.*

The site on which Carpenter's Kitchen stands really was used for a carpenter's workshop for almost a hundred years. When the last owner of the business, Arthur Olde, retired in 1987, his daughter, Debbie and her husband, Geoff Beszant recognised its potential as the perfect venue for a waterside tearoom. So, the Beszants restored the original building to house the kitchen and built a new wing from local stone to create what is now a thriving business. From the front door, there is a view over the harbour and inside, the wooden floor, polished tables and old photographs of the craftsmen who owned the business over the years make a comfortable, rural setting for delicious Cornish teas.

The accent is on traditional local food, all prepared on the premises. In the summer season, sandwiches and salads are generously filled with locally-caught crab, thick Cornish clotted cream can be dolloped on freshly-baked Cornish splits or scones and many of Debbie's cakes, including chocolate cakes and brown sugar meringues, are cooked to tried and tested, favourite family recipes. *Teas served:* House Blend (Imperial Tea, a blend of Kenya and India, specially blended to suit the local soft water), Earl Grey, Darjeeling, Assam, Lapsang Souchong. *Fruit teas and herbal infusions are also available.*

MAD HATTER'S

Owner: Victoria James

28 Church Street
Launceston, Cornwall
PL15 8AR
Tel: 01566 777188

Directions
Launceston is just off the A30 in north Cornwall.
Mad Hatter's is in the centre of the town, 30 yards
from the town square, opposite WH Smiths.

Opening times
Open all year except Christmas Day and
Boxing Day. Sundays, closed in winter.
Monday–Saturday, 10 am–5.30 pm.
Sunday, 11 am–4 pm (in summer only).

Local Interest:
Launceston is the ancient capital of Cornwall and there is
a Castle run by English Heritage, a museum and a Town
Trail which walks you past all the interesting landmarks
of the town.

Victoria James admits that being totally 'nutty' helped in creating this very idiosyncratic tea room where Lewis Carroll's characters are everywhere.

Victoria designed and decorated the shop herself and created the wonderfully humourous menu that offers Mad Hatter's Platters of cheese, tuna or smoked ham with bread and pickles, Alice's Scrumptious Sandwiches, March Hare's Marvellous Cakes and Mad Hatter Specials. The most popular item has to be the Indecisive Cake Taster whereby those tempted by several of the home-made calorie-laden gâteaux can sample any three, and those who simply cannot make up their minds at all can ask the waitresses to choose for them.

The tea is served in novelty teapots, and there are more unusual pots for sale and on display, including the special Dormouse teapot that was designed and hand-made for the shop by a Cornish potter.

Victoria is aware that her customers are sometimes shy of trying new and unusual teas, so she organises regular tea promotions to encourage them to taste those they don't know. *Teas served:* Assam, Ceylon, Darjeeling, Earl Grey, English Breakfast, Kenya, Lapsang Souchong, Mad Hatter's Special Blend (lightly spiced). *Scented teas and herbal infusions also available.*

THE PLANTATION CAFE

Owners: Ann and Maurice Vaughan

**The Coombes, Polperro
Cornwall PL13 2RG
Tel: 01503 272223**

Directions

Park in the main car park and walk to the Plantation Cafe which is on the right hand side of the main road, half way between the car park and the harbour.

Opening times
Open April–end September, except Saturdays.
Monday–Friday, 10.30 am–5.30 pm
(9 am in peak season).
Saturday, closed.
Sunday, 10.30 am–5.30 pm.

Local Interest:
Polperro is a traditional fishing village once well known for its smuggling. Visit the new Teglio museum that tells the history of Polperro and South East Cornwall and take a pleasure trip in a fishing boat to see the coves and the caves along the coast. Also look out for the stories about Piskeys, the Cornish fairy folk, and their Queen, Joan of Wad, and King Sam Spriggin.

In the vigorous days of Victorian expansion and enterprise, a local Polperro man went off adventuring in North America and made a fortune on the plantations there. He later returned to the place where he was born and used some of the money to build this black and white house right beside the River Pol – hence the name of the tearoom. The building stands in a conservation area so it's solid, secure Victorian exterior of traditional Cornish stone and Delabole slate roof will never change. Inside, the Victorian theme is continued with exposed black and white beams, an open fireplace with its copper hood, oak tables, wheelback chairs, copper and brass pots and pans and collections of teapots and Delft ware to decorate the walls.

The river runs peacefully alongside the lovingly-tended garden that has won awards for its beauty and colour and provides a stunning setting for lunch or tea. The menu offers all sorts of local specialities – Cornish pasties, cheese and onion pies, sandwiches made with locally caught crab, and delicious home-made cakes, scones and fruit pies served with Cornish clotted cream. Real traditional Cornish treats! *Teas served:* House Blend, Earl Grey, Assam, Darjeeling, Lapsang Souchong, Ceylon. *Fruit flavoured and herbal teas are also offered.*

RECTORY TEAROOMS

Owner: Jill Savage

**Rectory Farm, Morwenstow
Near Bude, Cornwall EX23 9SR
Tel: 01288 331251**

Directions
From the A39, from Bideford to Bude, turn off at the sign to Morwenstow. Follow signs to the village and church. The tearoom is next to the church.

Opening times
Open Easter–end October.
Monday–Thursday and Sunday, 11 am–6 pm.
Fridays and Saturdays, 11 am–6 pm and 7.30 pm–9.30 pm.

Local Interest:
Only ten minutes away is some of the most spectacular scenery in North Cornwall. Next door is the ancient Church of St John the Baptist and famous graveyard with the graves of shipwrecked sailors.

Rectory Farm has a long long history and is mentioned in a document dated 1296 when it belonged to the monks of St John of Bridgewater. The main hall of the house with its heavy oak beams and ancient stone flagged floor is now the restaurant and tearoom and has been run by the same family for some 40 years. It was the current owner, Jill Savage's mother-in-law, who set it up in 1954 when she realised that a lot of people were passing her door on their walks along the coastal footpath that runs right past the front door. She recognised the potential for a busy tearoom and created a warm, traditional interior with Victorian furniture and chintz curtains and today, there is a steady stream of customers right through the summer season. As well as enjoying high quality lunches, teas and dinners, you can buy local jams, chutneys and other produce from the little shop area.

Visitors come from all over the world to see the church of St John the Baptist, made famous by Parson Hawker, an eccentric who introduced Harvest Festival to British churches and wrote the famous Cornish anthem, 'Trelawney'. Rectory Farm, which is next door, gives them a chance to also enjoy a really good traditional English tea. *Teas served:* India, Earl Grey, Lapsang Souchong. *Herbal teas are also offered.*

THE COMMODORE HOTEL

Owner: Bruce Woolaway

Marine Parade
Instow, North Devon
EX39 4JN
Tel: 01271 860347
Fax: 01271 861233

Directions
From the M5 take Exit 27 for the North
Devon Link Road. Take the turning to Instow
signposted just before Torridge Bridge. Follow
signs for Instow seafront and these will bring
you to Marine Parade.

Opening times
Open to non-residents all year, 7.30 am–9.30 pm.
Tea is served from 3–6 pm.

Local Interest:
The historic towns of Bideford and Barnstaple are nearby
and Instow is within easy reach of Exmoor and Dartmoor
National parks.

Originally a Georgian gentleman's residence, this waterside hotel sits elegantly overlooking the mouth of the rivers Taw and Torridge in one of North Devon's prettiest locations. The Woolaways, a local Devon family, have owned the hotel since 1969 and they have created a stylish, welcoming environment where views of the palm trees, sweeping lawns that slope gently down to the sandy shore and the constantly changing waterfront scenery make it a perfect place for afternoon tea. In summer months, relax on the terrace and watch the yachts scudding by with billowing sails, and in the chillier winter months, take shelter from the sea breezes in the comfortable lounge.

The hotel's marine setting is echoed in the menu where a good range of seafoods is offered for lunchtime savouries and in open sandwiches. And, since this is the home of clotted cream, don't miss the cream tea, or, for a change, try a clotted cream ice cream or treat yourself to one of the rich desserts or cakes that are served with generous portions of either the clotted or double variety of the delicious indulgence. *Teas served:* Assam, Darjeeling, Lapsang Souchong, Earl Grey, Traditional PG Tips. *Flavoured teas and herbal infusions are also offered.*

38

THE COSY TEAPOT

Owners: Jean and Brian Chave

**13 Fore Street, Budleigh Salterton
Devon EX9 6NH
Tel: 01395 444016**

Directions
Budleigh Salterton is 11 miles from Junction 30 of the M5 and 4 miles east of Exmouth. The Cosy Teapot is situated at the lower end of the main street, towards the seafront.

Opening times
Open all year except Wednesday.
Monday, Tuesday, Thursday,
Friday, Saturday, Sunday,
10 am–5 pm in summer,
10 am–4.30 pm in winter.

Local Interest:
Sir Walter Raleigh's birth place is a couple of miles away and Milais' famous painting of Sir Walter on the sea wall is about 50 yards from the shop. The local museum specialises in old lace and there are cliff walks and wonderful surrounding countryside.

One of the reasons that Jean and Brian chose this particular shop is the little stream that runs right past the front door and which you have to cross by way of a small bridge to get inside. Once upon a time, in about 1880, this was the 'Library' and later a shoemender's shop. Now it is a delightful Victorian style tea-room and inside, you will find a colourful array of about 70 teapots that have been collected by Jean over the past few years and an atmosphere that reminds a lot of visitors of 'Miss Marples'.

Jean's passion for teapots means that not only does the shop have a display of old, new and novelty pots but sells some novelty pots as well. While your eyes take in the variety and colourful details, the friendly and efficient staff will bring you a Cosy Teapot Special Cream Tea that the Chaves serve with a tea cake instead of the traditional scones. And, of course, there's lots of clotted cream and jam. Of all the cakes on the menu that are baked specially for the shop, the most popular are the apple cake that is served warm with cream and the fruit cake made by Brian's mum. *Teas served:* House Blend, Assam, Darjeeling, Earl Grey.

COURT BARN COUNTRY HOUSE HOTEL

Owners: Susan and Robert Wood

Clawton, Holsworthy
Devon EX22 6PS
Tel: 01409 271219
Fax: 01409 271309

Directions
Clawton is 2½ miles south of Holsworthy off the A388 (from Bude to Launceston). Court Barn is next to Clawton's 12th century church.

Opening times
Open all year except the first week of January. Monday–Sunday, 10 am–5.30 pm.

Awards
1987 & 89   Tea Council Award of Excellence
Egon Ronay recommended

Local Interest:
Clawford Vineyard, several local nature trails, Cookworthy Woods, sailing on Roadford and Tomao Lakes, Holsworthy Pannier Market (Wednesday). A short drive to Bude and National Trust beaches and coastal walks.

Court Barn is a charming Victorian House, rebuilt in 1853 from a 16th century manor house known as Court Baron. The hotel stands in five acres of beautiful tranquil park-like gardens hidden amongst rolling Devon countryside and close to the spectacular National Trust and English Heritage coastline.

The house is filled with antiques, paintings and decorative objects. Fresh flowers fill the elegant dining rooms and lounges and there is a crackling log fire in the cosy bar, creating a warm, friendly and relaxed atmosphere. And on balmy summer days, the garden makes an idyllic setting for a special Devon clotted cream tea with one of the 45 teas on the menu. For the more energetic, there is croquet, lawn tennis and badminton or gentle strolls around the garden.

The menu is crammed with wonderful home-baked sweets and savouries, soups and patés, vegetarian dishes, sandwiches and cakes such as Marsala and Almond, Honey and Cherry, Chocolate and Walnut. Home cooking at its best! *Teas served:* House Blends (India/Ceylon, India/Kenya), Indian, Darjeeling, Darjeeling and Ceylon, Assam, Kenya, Lapsang Souchong, Earl Grey, Pure China Oolong, Keemun, Rose Pouchong, Gunpowder, Broken Orange Pekoe, English Breakfast. *Fruit flavoured and herbal teas are also offered.*

FOUR & TWENTY BLACKBIRDS

Owner: Jaqueline Webb

43 Gold Street, Tiverton
Devon EX16 6QB
Tel: 01884 257055

Directions
From the M5 take Exit 27, Exeter to Taunton,
then take the A373 to Tiverton.

Opening times
Open all year except Sundays.
Monday–Saturday, 9 am–5.30 pm.
Sunday, closed.

Local Interest:
Tiverton's 11th century Castle was built by commission of
Henry I and the ruins now house the interesting Campbell
Clock Collection. The 700-year-old church has some
beautiful carvings and the award-winning Museum
contains a lot of railway memorabilia, including the last
steam engine to run in the area, affectionately known as
the Tivvy Bumper. There are also 11 miles of walks along
the banks of the canal and horse-drawn barge rides.

The theme of this totally charming tea shop is the famous nursery rhyme 'Sing a Song of Six Pence'. All the characters from the song are there on the menu – the blackbirds, the King in his counting house, the Queen in the parlour and the maid who was perpetually hanging out the clothes in the garden. The King's choice is savoury – a robust tea with a wholemeal roll, cheddar cheese, chutney and salad – while the Queen delights in sweetmeats and a light tea of boiled egg with bread and butter. The maid's tea is homemade apple pie with clotted Devonshire cream, cheese or ice cream.

Both the outside and inside of the shop (that also sells antiques) are as attractive and appealing as the creative ideas on the menu. The windows – full of porcelain teapots, stoneware jars, jam pots and other tablewares – are dressed with hanging baskets that cascade colour, and once inside, the eye is drawn to lots more interesting objects – baskets, brass trays, decorative plates – that fill the walls and surround the open fireplace. And the array of food on display on the counter and trolley is mouthwatering. Everything is home-made, including the jams, so step into the nostalgic nursery rhyme world of years gone by and indulge in a wonderful traditional tea. *Teas served:* Ceylon, Darjeeling, Assam, Earl Grey, Lapsang Souchong. *Herbal teas are also offered.*

GREYS DINING ROOM

Owners: David Winstone and
Gary Dowland

**96 High Street, Totnes
Devon TQ9 5SN
Tel: 01803 866369**

Directions
Greys is situated in 'The Narrows' at the top of the High Street opposite the Post Office.

Opening times
Open all year except Wednesdays.
Monday, Tuesday, Thursday & Saturday,
10 am–5 pm. Friday, 9.30 am–5 pm.
Sunday, 12 noon–5 pm. Wednesday, closed.

Awards
1993, 94 & 95 Tea Council Award of Excellence

Local Interest:
Totnes has an Elizabethan museum, Norman Castle and 17th century Guildhall. Boats go from here to Dartmouth and steam trains will take you up the Dart Valley to Buckfastleigh. From May to the end of September, there is an Elizabethan market every Tuesday in the Market Square and Rotherfold Square.

Local archives have proved Totnes to be the oldest borough in England and the very pretty town is full of beautiful Elizabethan and Georgian architecture. As you approach the elegant Georgian facade of Greys Dining Room, your eyes will be drawn by the old iron urns in the window that hold graceful ferns and, arranged around them in one window, attractive antique tablewares that are for sale. In the other window, home-made cakes invite you to step down into the old world charm of the 250-year-old building that once housed an olde fashioned sweet shop.

Just inside the door, more wonderful cakes are displayed in an antique Flemish glass and wood cabinet that is carved with cherubs and fruits and shows the cakes off to perfection. All around are colourful saucers on the walls, antique furniture, pictures and copper pots.

While you enjoy the classic beauty of the decorative items, treat yourself to tea time traditionals such as crumpets, toasted teacakes and scones with local Devonshire clotted cream and then, if you can make up your mind which to choose, indulge in one of the 20 or so cakes. *Teas served:* House Blend, Earl Grey, Darjeeling, Indian Prince, Assam, Keemun, Lapsang Souchong. *Fruit flavoured and herbal teas are also offered.*

THE PARLOUR

Owners: Susan and Philip Hungate

112 East Street, South Molton
Devon EX36 3DB
Tel: 01769 574144

Directions
South Molton is signposted off the North
Devon Link Road that runs off the M5. The
Parlour, with its swinging sign, is on the main
road through the town.

Opening times
Open all year except Sundays & Mondays.
Tuesday–Saturday, 10 am–5.30 pm. 🚭

Local Interest:
South Molton is known for its antique shops selling lace,
pine, paintings, etc, and for the livestock market on
Thursdays and Pannier Market on Thursdays and
Saturdays. Also visit the Quince Honey Farm.

As you pass under the traditional fanlight above the doorway of this very attractive double fronted Georgian house, you feel immediately as if you have stepped into Susan and Philip Hungate's front room. A grandfather clock ticks reassuringly in the corner, the walls are deep Georgian green and red and the open fire and warm red of the carpet give a richness and depth to the tearoom. A plate rack runs high up around the walls and displays green Wedgwood plates, and there is an amusing collection of gollys and Victorian dolls that started with Susan's own golly and was added to by customers with similar lonely toys.

All the breads, cakes, scones and biscuits are home-made and Susan's range of cakes mixes firm favourites such as apple cake and coffee and walnut with other scrumptious treats such as rich chocolate cake, sticky ginger cake, date and walnut and traditional English cheesecake. Or you can indulge in real traditional tea-time specials such as boiled eggs with soldier boys, cinnamon toast, sardines on toast or real Welsh or Buck Rarebit. A wonderful parlour tea! *Teas served:* Assam, Darjeeling, Earl Grey, Lapsang Souchong, Keemun.

LEWIS'S TEA-ROOMS

Owners: Ron and Annie Baker

13 The High Street, Dulverton
Somerset TA22 9HB
Tel: 01398 323850

Directions
Dulverton is on the A3223 that runs from
north west to south east across Exmoor. It is 14
miles north of Tiverton and 25 miles south of
Minehead.

Opening times
Open all year.
Monday–Saturday, 9.30 am–5.30 pm.
Sunday, 10.30 am–5.30 pm.

Local Interest:
Set on the southern edge of Exmoor, Dulverton is ideally
placed for exploring the area and for visits to Somerset's
coastal towns.

Set in the High Street of this attractive Exmoor town, Lewis's Tea-Rooms offers the ideal stopping off point. The pretty room has a wooden floor, two open fireplaces which burn brightly with log fires in the winter months, lots of paintings and pictures (some by the owner), fresh flowers, decorative plates and jugs and an amusing collection of brush ducks! The tables are covered with charming floral or lace cloths under sparkling glass table tops.

The tea menu offers a choice of cream teas, the Exmoor, the Dulverton, the West Country or the Somerset – all varied according to taste and appetite – and an irresistible selection of home-made cakes which are prominently displayed on the centre table.

Full English breakfasts are available and, at lunchtime, a tempting choice of home-made soups, pies (savoury and sweet) and crumbles is available alongside other traditional teashop treats.

The counter in the corner displays a selection of home-made jams and marmalades, and the window is filled with very attractive cake stands and chinawares. *Teas served:* Typhoo Original, Earl Grey, Darjeeling, Assam, Lapsang Souchong. *Herbal teas are also offered.*

THE TEA SHOPPE
AND RESTAURANT

Owners: Pam and Norman Goldsack

3 High Street, Dunster
Somerset, TA24 6SF
Tel: 01643 821304

Directions
The Tea Shoppe is situated near the traffic lights in the High Street, by the entrance to Dunster Castle.

Opening times
November, December open weekends only.
March–end October, Monday, Tuesday,
Wednesday, Friday, Saturday, Sunday,
10 am–5.30 pm or later. Thursday, closed.

Awards
1989, 90 & 94 Tea Council Award of Excellence

Local Interest:
Dunster is a medieval town that was once important in the cotton trade. Visit Dunster Castle, St George's Church and Priory, the working water mill and enjoy walks in the surrounding countryside.

Pam and Norman Goldsack came to Dunster from Yorkshire in 1984 and took over the tea shop that had been established here since the 1930s. With a real feel for local specialities, they upgraded it to a restaurant and tearoom and now serve an excellent range of high quality savouries and sweets, including freshly baked rustic breads and cakes made with local produce. The West Country Treacle Tart, Somerset Cider and Bramley Apple cakes are too good to miss, and if you are there for lunch, try the unbelievable bread and butter pudding made with clotted cream – one of 10 or 12 puddings on the menu each day. Pam bakes in an Aga throughout the day and so, at tea time, the scones come to your table as fresh and warm as you will ever find.

The two tearooms are in what were once three little 15th century cottages which retain many of their original features. The roofs are made from the pil reed that grows locally on the Dunster marshes, and the low beams create a comfortable, cottage feel which the Goldsacks have enhanced with country furniture and flowered curtains and wallpaper. The friendly, thoughtful service and delicious food make this a popular venue for visitors from all over the world. *Teas served:* Tea Shoppe Blend, Keemun, Lapsang Souchong, Earl Grey, Darjeeling, Assam, Ceylon. *Fruit flavoured and herbal teas are also offered.*

THE BRIDGE TEA ROOMS

Owners: Francine and Richard Whale

**24A Bridge Street, Bradford-on-Avon
Wiltshire BA15 1BY
Tel: 01225 865537**

Directions
Turn immediately left after going over the old town bridge and park in the free town car park. Walk out of the car park and the tearooms are situated just across the narrow street in front of you.

Opening times
Open all year except Christmas Day and Boxing Day. Monday–Saturday, 9.30 am–5.30 pm. Sunday, 10.30 am–5.30 pm.

Awards
1994   Tea Council Award of Excellence
Egon Ronay recommended

Local Interest:
Visit the 12th century Saxon church and the tithe barn with its stone tiled roof that is said to be the largest in England, or walk along the canal and enjoy the undulating countryside of the surrounding Wiltshire countryside.

Although the building that houses the Bridge Tea Rooms was constructed in 1675, the interior has been themed in Victorian style with aspidistras, 19th century china and memorabilia, including busts of Queen Victoria herself, and sepia photographs of local views and past relatives of the current owners, Francine and Richard Whale. The waitresses costumes recall the early days of London's first tearooms when white frilly aprons were worn over black dresses and white mob caps covered curls and topknots. The ambience and service are delightful, and the food is excellent.

A full afternoon tea includes sandwiches, a crumpet, a scone with thick Devon clotted cream and jam, and a cake. But if you just want a cup of tea and something sweet, there is a wide choice of really luscious cakes and patisseries that come fresh from the oven. Try a slice of carrot, banana and walnut, or choose one of the roulades – Belgian chocolate, fresh strawberry, lemon, hazelnut or pineapple and coconut. *Teas served:* House Blend, Earl Grey, Darjeeling FOP, Assam, Lapsang Souchong, Ceylon BOP, Ceylon Orange Pekoe, Kenya, Pelham, First Flush Darjeeling, Jasmine. *Fruit flavoured teas are also offered.*

POLLY TEA ROOMS

Owner: Julian West

**26–27 High Street, Marlborough
Wiltshire SN8 1LW
Tel: 01672 512146**

Directions
**Marlborough is on the A4. Polly's is half way
along the High Street.**

Opening times
Open all year.
Monday–Friday, 8.30 am–6 pm.
Saturday, 8 am–7 pm. Sunday, 9 am–7 pm.

Awards
1985   Tea Council Top Tea Place of The Year
Egon Ronay recommended

Local Interest:
*The very pretty mainly Georgian High Street is a good
hunting ground for antiques and half-timbered houses in
some of the back streets are very attractive. St Peter's Church
has a craft centre. Nearby, visit Avebury Stone Circle and
climb Silbury Hill for panoramic views of the area.*

Polly's is probably one of the most important tourist attractions in Marlborough and everyone who has tea here says how wonderful it is. The shop is in a very fine bow-windowed 17th century building that was originally a house and there has been a tea shop here for over 50 years. As you walk through to the large, beamed tearoom, you are bound to be tempted by the mouthwatering array of chocolates and pastries on the counter just inside the entrance. Everything is made on the premises by local pastry chefs and you'll find it hard to decide what to choose from the long list of possibilities – macaroons, rum truffles, date slice, lemon and redcurrant cheesecake, muesli scones, Danish pastries and lots more.

Once you have made your decision, sit back and enjoy the traditional setting with its pretty flowered China, pine dressers, lace tablecloths and neatly uniformed girls who are busy all day serving tourists, schoolboys from nearby Marlborough College and their parents, and local customers who find this the perfect place to sit and relax. *Teas served:* Indian, Earl Grey, Lapsang Souchong. *Fruit infusion is also offered.*

S O U T H   E A S T
R E G I O N A L   M A P

CLARA'S

Owner: Jane Seabrook

9 High Street, East Hoathly
Near Lewes
East Sussex BN8 6DR
Tel: 01825 840339

Directions
East Hoathly is just off the A22 south of
Uckfield. Clara's is in the centre of the village.

Opening times
Open all year except Mondays, Tuesdays and
two weeks 24th December—mid-January.
Monday—Tuesday, closed.
Wednesday—Saturday, 10.30 am—5 pm.
Sunday, 2—5 pm.

Local Interest:
*East Hoathly has a pottery, a shop called "Specially For
You" which sells high-quality hand-made smocked
garments and the old petrol station is converted to a craft
workshop where furniture makers and restorers, saddlers
and other crafts people work and sell their goods.*

The owner of this pretty tea shop, Jane Seabrook, is very interested in the history of her village and·researches the family trees and histories of local village people. East Hoathly was the home of Thomas Turner, diarist and local shopkeeper and Jane sells copies of his writings which chronicle his life in the late 1700s and give a rare and detailed insight into village life in those days. Clara's itself dates from the same period, but has a Victorian facade, and inside, there are oak beams and an inglenook fireplace. In good weather, there is extra seating outside.

Upstairs, there is a very interesting permanent exhibition of knitting, sewing and related memorabilia such as old sewing tools and knitting patterns and the shop sells tapestry kits, knitting yarns, pretty cards, Sussex honey and local home-made chutneys, jams and jellies. The chutney also appears on the menu to accompany delicious rolls filled with chicken, cheese, egg mayonnaise or smoked salmon. The cake selection includes gingerbread, walnut cake and coffee sponge and teas are locally packaged. *Teas served:* Traditional Blend, Earl Grey, Darjeeling. *Herbal teas are also offered.*

PAVILION TEA ROOMS

Owners: Coastline Caterers on behalf of Eastbourne Borough Council

**Royal Parade, Eastbourne
East Sussex BN22 7AQ
Tel: 01323 410374**

Directions
The Pavilion Tea Rooms is situated on the seafront, half a mile east of the pier towards the Sovereign Centre.

Opening times
Open all year.
In Summer, Monday–Sunday, 10 am–9 pm.
In Winter, Monday–Sunday, 10 am–5 pm.

Local Interest:
Visit the Towner Art Gallery and Museum, the Butterfly Centre on the seafront, the Lifeboat Museum, the Museum of Shops, the pier and the Napoleonic fortress. Also good for walks along the seafront and to Beachy Head.

What could be more reminiscent of Victorian and Edwardian tea times at the seaside than to sip Lapsang Souchong on the patio tea terrace or laze over a pot of Darjeeling in the tea rooms whilst enjoying the stunning vista across the bay to Beachy Head. The setting and the style recreate everyone's idea of all the essential elements of a memorable English tea – a light and elegant room with a view, waiters who calmly bring you everything you could possibly want, newspapers for browsing through, the gentle music of the piano on summer afternoons and evenings and winter weekends, and a menu absolutely crammed with wonderful ideas to suit all tastes, all times of the year and all weathers. You may choose to tuck into a cinnamon muffin or nibble at a slice of traditional chocolate fudge cake, dip a long spoon into a toffee and brandy snap sundae that oozes ice cream, cream and toffee sauce, or enjoy an old-fashioned Sussex Cream Tea.

The gift shop also sells vouchers which can be exchanged for afternoon tea or souvenirs. *Teas served:* Pavilion Blend, Earl Grey, Lapsang Souchong, China Rose Congou, Estate Assam, Ceylon Orange Pekoe, Estate Darjeeling, Jasmine. *Fruit flavoured and herbal teas are also offered.*

COBWEB TEAROOMS

Owner: Angela Webley

**49 The Hundred, Romsey
Hampshire SO51 8GE
Tel: 01794 516434**

Directions

Follow signs to Romsey off M27 or M3. Cobweb Tearooms is the last shop at the end of the main street, a few doors from Waitrose and 100 yards from the main entrance to Broadlands.

Opening times
Open all year except two weeks at the end of September and one week at Christmas.
Monday, closed except Bank Holidays.
Tuesday–Saturday, 10 am–5.30 pm.
Sunday, closed except Bank Holidays.
Bank Holiday Sundays, 2.30–5.30 pm. 🚭

Local Interest:
From the tea shop, it is only a short walk to Broadlands (where Lord Mountbatten lived), the Norman Abbey, King John's House and a Hunting Lodge. Hillier's Arboretum is three or four miles away and a 15 minute drive south takes you into the heart of the New Forest.

The old-world ambience of Cobweb Tearooms is exactly right for its setting in Romsey – a charming little town with interesting antique shops and quaint old streets on its edges, where Georgian and Victorian houses stand surrounded by picturesque gardens. Angela Webley has established a popular, friendly environment where locals regularly pop in for a refreshing cuppa after a shopping trip and where visitors stop off on their way to the New Forest or after a visit to Broadlands, the home of Lord Romsey.

The comfortable tearoom is in a half-timbered, late 17th century building that was once an old-fashioned cobblers and shoe shop. The outside is decorated with generously-filled hanging baskets that add a lovely splash of colour to the white walls. The paved garden at the back provides more seating and is filled with flowers – a delightful spot in which to sample some of Angela's home baking. The trolley is laden with pavlovas, chocolate hazelnut torte, carrot cake and chocolate gâteau, and in winter, there are always hot puds such as sticky toffee pudding to warm you and fill you up. *Teas served:* Traditional Typhoo, Nairobi, Assam, Darjeeling, English Breakfast, Earl Grey, Lapsang Souchong. *Herbal teas are also offered, including mango and camomile.*

SEA COTTAGE TEA SHOPPE

Owners: Wendy & Kevin Noon

**Marine Drive
Barton-on-Sea
Hampshire BH25 7DZ
Tel: 01425 614086**

Directions

Travelling south through the New Forest, follow the Lymington road to New Milton where there are signposts to Barton-on-Sea. Keep on this road until you see Sea Cottage Tea Shoppe on the edge of the cliff, overlooking Christchurch Bay.

Opening times

Open February–end December.
Monday, closed.
Tuesday–Sunday, 10 am–5 pm.

Local Interest:

The New Forest and the coastline provide miles of beautiful countryside for walks, cycling and horse-riding. Christchurch and Beaulieu are not far away and, to the east, lies Hurst Castle.

Kevin Noon used to serve teas on board the QE2 and this and the marine setting for the cliff-top tea shop has led to a menu with a slightly nautical theme. In the middle of the day, you can feast on the 'Captain's' lunch, and there's a 'Pirates' menu for kids. The cream tea is called 'High Tide' and a set tea of sandwiches and cakes is aptly named 'Full Sail', while 'Half Mast' is scones on their own. Everything is home-made and Wendy and Kevin have won New Forest District Council's awards for their no smoking policy and their healthy cooking. But, don't worry, that doesn't mean that favourite tea-time treats are not available – there are chocolate truffles, apricot and fruit cake, walnut and chocolate sponge and lots more.

Letters of appreciation from past customers bear testimony to the warm welcome, the high standards and friendly service that is given by both Kevin and Wendy. One note says: "We would like to thank you for those excellent lunches, the variety on the menu and not least the happy smiling attention given to us by Wendy. . . . For Kevin, whom we seldom saw, but will be remembered for his culinary skills, our appreciation for all his products." *Teas served:* House Blend, Earl Grey, Darjeeling, Assam, Lapsang Souchong, Lemon, Decaffeinated. *Flavoured teas and herbal infusions are also offered.*

THATCHED COTTAGE HOTEL & RESTAURANT

Owners: Margaret, Matthias, Martin and Michiyo Matysik

16 Brookley Road
Brockenhurst, New Forest
Hampshire SO42 7RR
Tel: 01590 623090
Fax: 01590 623479

Directions
Brockenhurst is in the heart of the New Forest on the A337 and B3055. The hotel is located on the road into the village centre, a few minutes walk from the railway station.

Opening times
Open all year except Mondays and 5th–31st January. Monday, closed. Tuesday–Sunday, 2.30–5.30 pm.

Local Interest:
The New Forest has facilities for walking, cycling, golf, horse riding, sailing and fishing.

The 400-year-old thatched cottage was built in 1627 before anyone in England had heard about tea. The Matysik family took over the hotel and tearoom in 1989 and have brought a modern, international flavour to their cuisine, but have kept the old world enchantment and charm. Canaries sing in the tearoom which is filled with antiques, rugs, decorative objects from around the world and arrangements of fresh and dried flowers. The tea garden has cushions, parasols and lace tablecloths to create a sense of luxury and elegance.

Afternoon tea here is a real treat. There is an imaginative selection of sandwiches and the cakes and desserts are equally tempting – they range from traditional English recipes to foreign specialities such as Apple Strudel, Sachertorte, American cheesecakes and Swiss ice creams. The Complete Cream Tea is incredibly good value and consists of finger sandwiches, three varieties of scone (plain, fruited and wholemeal with walnut) served with very generous portions of jam and clotted cream, a selection of pastries and cakes and a pot of tea. Not surprisingly, people travel from far and wide for such indulgence. *Teas served:* Earl Grey, Assam, Lapsang Souchong, Darjeeling, English Breakfast, Brooke Bond Special Blend, Decaffeinated. *Herbal teas are also offered.*

CLARIS'S

Owners: Brian and Janet Wingham

1–3 High Street, Biddenden
Kent TN27 8AL
Tel: 01580 291025

Directions

Biddenden lies at the junction of the A274 and A262, 12 miles south of Maidstone. The tearoom is in the centre of the village opposite the village green.

Opening times
Open all year except Mondays.
Monday, closed.
Tuesday–Sunday, 10.30 am–5.20 pm.

Award
Egon Ronay recommended

Local Interest:
Within the village, strolling visitors can discover the story of the Biddenden maids who were born joined at the hip and shoulders in 1100 and lived like that for 34 years, refusing to be separated. There are also fine examples of medieval to 17th century architecture and a 13th century church whose school is said to be haunted.

A row of picturesque 15th century weavers' houses graces the gentle bend in the unspoilt main street of this quiet Kentish village that was once the centre of the cloth trade. At the east end of the row stands Claris's tearoom and gift shop with its windows temptingly filled with porcelain and pottery, jewellery and other gifts from the selection inside, and its arched porchway that leads into the old world charm of the shop and tearoom. The low oak beams and the two inglenook fireplaces create an atmosphere of homely cosiness where lace tablecloths cover spacious tables and delicious home-baked cakes and savouries are served on pretty white china.

Having settled at your table, it may take you quite a while to decide between the lemon madeira, the walnut bread served with apricot preserve, the hot bread pudding or Claris's cointreau cake that is covered with oodles of whipped double cream from a local dairy. Or you may decide that a Scottish smoked salmon or prawn sandwich is the ideal accompaniment to your afternoon cup of tea. Whatever you choose, this is the perfect place to relax after a wander around Biddenden village or a ramble in the nearby Wealden countryside. *Teas served:* House Kenya Blend, Earl Grey, Darjeeling, Lapsang Souchong and Assam. *Fruit flavoured and herbal teas are also offered.*

THE VILLAGE TEASHOP

Owner: David Aitchison

3 The Village
Chiddingstone, Edenbridge
Kent TN8 7AH
Tel: 01892 870326
Fax: 01892 870326

Directions
The tea shop is in the centre of Chiddingstone, which lies between Tonbridge and Edenbridge on the B2027.

Opening times
Open February–end November.
Closed December–end January.
Mondays, open only by request.
Tuesday–Sunday, 11 am–5.30 pm.

Local Interest:
The Village Shop dates back to some time between 1621 and 1636 and has been in uninterrupted business for over 350 years. The Post Office is even older. Chiddingstone Castle is open to the public and the Chiding Stone is a short walk away, down a narrow footpath near the school house.

Chiddingstone is one of the prettiest villages in Kent, with its beautiful old timbered Tudor buildings, its authentic Elizabethan atmosphere, its castle and lovely church. Surrounded by some of Britain's most beautiful, gently rolling countryside, the village looks today almost exactly as it did in the reign of Queen Elizabeth I and the tea shop is set in the very heart of one of the most important mansions in the village of that time. Burghersh Court once belonged to a nobleman by the name of Sir Thomas Bullen whose daughter, Ann (Boleyn), became Queen of England and one of Henry VIII's less fortunate wives since she subsequently lost her head for failing to produce a son and heir.

It is the Old Coach House of Burghersh Court that now houses the charming Village Teashop. Here, amidst the rich history of centuries of village life, visitors can take morning coffee, lunch or afternoon tea. The menu offers such traditional treats as toasted tea-cakes, hot buttered toast and scones with jam and local cream, and the delicious cakes vary according to season. *Teas served:* Earl Grey, Darjeeling, Assam, Lapsang Souchong, Ceylon, Traditional PG Tips. *Herbal teas are also offered.*

THE DORCHESTER

THE PROMENADE

Manager: Elayne Appleby

**Park Lane, London
W1A 2HJ
Tel: 0171 629 8888
Fax: 0171 495 7351**

Directions
**The Dorchester is half way up Park Lane.
Nearest tube, Marble Arch.**

Opening times
Open all year.
Monday–Sunday, 8 am–1 pm.

Award
Egon Ronay recommended

Local Interest:
*Park Lane is very close to Mayfair, Oxford Street and
Hyde Park so there are shops, cinemas, walks, restaurants
and tourist attractions.*

Tea at the Dorchester is quite spectacular. No-one can fail to enjoy the elegant, yet leisurely, surroundings where marble pillars, exquisite carpets, stately plants and magnificent flowers in fine vases and planters and amazingly comfortable sofas and armchairs create around you a sense of total calm and refinement. Despite such grand style, the extremely friendly staff make sure you are relaxed and comfortable and have everything you need. The opulence of the occasion recalls the style of the very first Afternoon Teas that took place at the beginning of the 19th century in palaces and stately homes around England.

Tea in The Promenade is brought one course at a time – first the neat finger sandwiches, then the scones with Devonshire clotted cream and jam and finally pastries freshly made by the restaurant's patissier. Second and third servings are always offered but it is doubtful whether many will be able to accept further indulgences. For special occasions, choose a glass of Dorchester champagne to accompany the delicious food. *Teas served:* Dorchester House Blend, Earl Grey, Darjeeling, Assam, China Keemun, Lapsang Souchong, China Caravan, China Oolong, Jasmine, English Breakfast, Russian Caravan. *Fruit flavoured and herbal teas are also offered.*

LE MERIDIEN PICCADILLY

OAK ROOM TEA LOUNGE

Manager: Alice Power

21 Piccadilly
London W1V 0BH
Tel: 0171 734 8000, ext 2309
Fax: 0171 437 3574

Directions
Le Meridien Hotel is at the Piccadilly Circus end of Piccadilly, just along the road from the Royal Academy and Burlington Arcade. Take the underground to Piccadilly Circus on the Piccadilly or Bakerloo line.

Opening times
The Oak Room is open all year from 10 am–11.30 pm.
Tea is served from 3–6 pm.

Local Interest:
All around Piccadilly and nearby Regent Street there are high quality shops, and not far away is Piccadilly Circus with its famous statue of Eros, Green Park, Trafalgar Square, the Mall and Buckingham Palace.

Le Meridien have been running this hotel since 1986 and have restored the Oak Room Lounge to its former Edwardian glory. The style is gracious and elegant and the soothing calm of the oak panelled room is heightened by extremely comfortable armchairs, which you just sink into, and the gentle music played by the resident harpist. Four wonderful Venetian clear glass chandeliers with twinkling candle bulbs cast a magical glow, while subdued side lamps give a rosy warmth to individual tables.

The very refined afternoon tea arrives on a silver and porcelain cake stand which is carefully laid with neat finger sandwiches of salmon, cream cheese and chives, egg and cheese, warm scones fresh from the oven and little jars of jam to accompany the clotted cream. And then there are the dainty continental-style pastries! Take time off from sightseeing or shopping and enjoy a truly delightful tea. *Teas served:* English Breakfast, Assam, Earl Grey, Darjeeling, Ceylon, Orange Pekoe, Lapsang Souchong, Keemun, Gunpowder, China Oolong, Yunnan, Formosa Oolong, Japanese Sencha, Pelham Blend, Russian Caravan, Decaffeinated Earl Grey and Ceylon. *Fruit flavoured and herbal teas are also offered.*

LE PAPILLON PATISSERIE

Owners: Chris & Harpal Pollard

249 Muswell Hill, Broadway
London N10
Tel: 0181 372 7156

Directions
The nearest tubes are Highgate and East Finchley on the Northern Line, and Bounds Green on the Piccadilly Line. From any of these, the shop is a 5 minute bus ride away. Main bus routes are the 134, 102 and 43.

Opening times
Open all year except Sundays, Mondays, Christmas and the last week in August. Tuesday–Saturday, 10 am–5 pm

Local Interest:
Alexandra Palace and Kenwood House are both very near, and 5 minutes away, Highgate Wood, Queens Wood and Hampstead Heath are fantastic for walking.

Harpal and Chris Pollard both have a deep interest in French patisserie and so when they decided to expand their bakery business to include a tearoom, it was natural that it should take on a French character and serve fine French cakes and pastries. Customers used to ask for a place to sit and enjoy some of the bakery's wonderful creations, so the Pollards made a space for them and now present everything with extreme care and exquisite taste in a very French ambience. There are old French chairs, a large 16th century French painting that creates a focal point, luxurious bright orange curtains, bought in Paris, which match the silk skirts worn by the hostesses. It is refreshing to find a decor so different, so special and so elegant and to enjoy such incredibly fine patisserie.

The cakes include divine almond flavoured 'Operas' – 8 layers of almond sponge, chocolate ganache, coffee butter cream and coffee syrup! An orange version tempts almost as much! And they make all their own breads, including baguettes and continental seeded breads, croissants and pains aux raisins, which are sold along with the fabulous range of cakes at the front counter. *Teas served:* English Breakfast, Assam, Darjeeling, Earl Grey, Lapsang Souchong, Jasmine. *Herbal infusions are also offered.*

THE TEA HOUSE

Owner: Su Russell

**College Farm
45 Fitzalan Road
London N3 3PG
Tel: 0171 240 9571
Fax: 0171 836 3893**

Directions
**The nearest tube station is Finchley Central.
Turn left out of the station, walk to the end of** the road and turn left into Regents Park Road.
Walk about ¼ mile and turn right into Fitzalan
Road. By road, turn off the North Circular
Road at Henlys Corner (junction with Finchley
Road) into Regents Park Road. Fitzalan Road is
off to the left.

Opening times
Open every Sunday, 2–6 pm.
Selected tea parties on other days.

Local Interest:
*College Farm still has cattle, sheep, pigs, goats, poultry,
donkeys, etc. Entrance charge: Adults £1.25, Children 70p,
Concessions £1.*

There has been a farm on this site since medieval times. Originally a sheep farm, it was bought in 1868 by the founder of the Express Dairy, G. T. Barham, who redesigned it in 1882 as a working dairy. In 1920, the dairy was turned into a tearoom but sadly, by the early 1980s, had become a rather shabby refreshments room. Then Su Russell became involved and she spent many lonely hours scraping determinedly at the seven layers of paint and paper that concealed the old Minton tiles. Working from a 1920s photograph, she has restored the room to its original charm, with bentwood chairs, chequered floor and tables decorated with linen cloths and fresh flowers.

It has taken Su years to collect the distinctive Willow Pattern tea services and treasures have been given by friends and customers, or hunted out from antique shops. Other 'finds' that add to the feel of nostalgia have been gratefully accepted – Express Dairy tea-towels, an old till and an early ice-cream maker. Now Su serves home-made scones with jam and Devon clotted cream (sent up by train every Sunday from Budleigh Salterton) in this delightful little time warp. *Teas served:* Indian, China, teas from Russia, Malawi, Thailand, Egypt, Singapore, Japan, Decaffeinated. *Fruit and herbal infusions are also offered.*

THE WALDORF
PALM COURT

Palm Court Manager: Arnauld Baert

**Aldwych, London
WC2B 4DD
Tel: 0171 836 2400
Fax: 0171 836 7244**

Directions
Nearest tube stations are Holborn or Charing

Cross. Buses that go to Aldwych are: 1, 9, 11, 13, 15, 23, 26, 68, 76, 77A, 91, 168, 171, 171A, 188, 501, 505, 521.

Opening times
Open all year.
Tea is served every day, 3.30–6 pm.

Local Interest:
Covent Garden, Royal Opera House, several major theatres, the City of London, and a short walk away over Waterloo Bridge lies the South Bank complex with concert halls, art galleries, theatres and museums.

The Waldorf Hotel opened its doors in 1908 and very quickly became a favourite place for an elegant and refined afternoon tea. In 1910 the Tango arrived from Buenos Aires and prompted the beginning of that rather eccentric mix of Argentine Dancing and English tea drinking – the Tea Dance. By 1913, the Waldorf's golden and white ballroom was one of London's most popular venues for Tango Tea Dances.

Today, tea is served in the magnificent Palm Court where exotic plants, a marble terrace, gentle Edwardian colours and twinkling lights create a unique setting for a very stylish tea. The menu suggests a variety of set teas – the traditional Palm Court Afternoon Tea offers sandwiches, warm scones with preserves and Devonshire clotted cream and a range of cakes and small pastries. For special occasions, the Waldorf Celebration Tea adds a glass of champagne and a special Celebration Cake, and each season brings its own variations. Tea Dances take place every Saturday and Sunday from 3.30–6 pm. *Teas served:* Assam, Ceylon, Darjeeling, Waldorf Blend, Earl Grey, Jasmine, Keemun, Lapsang Souchong, China Oolong, Rose Pouchong, minted iced tea. *Also available: Camomile, Peppermint, Rosehip and Hibiscus herbal infusions.*

GUILDFORD HOUSE TEA ROOM

Owner: Maureen Debenham

**155 High Street
Guildford
Surrey GU1 3AJ
Tel: 01483 454608**

Directions
Guildford House is in the main cobbled traffic-free High Street, opposite Sainsburys.

Opening times
Open all year except Sundays and Mondays.
Sunday and Monday, closed.
Tuesday–Saturday, 10 am–4.30 pm.

Local Interest:
From Guildford House, walk to the castle whose grounds are a treat, the Guildhall with its huge clock, the town's museum and several interesting churches.

Guildford House was built in 1660, at just the same time that the first cargoes of tea were arriving in the docks of London. The building was originally a private family house but was later altered to accommodate a shop on the ground floor and has, over the years, housed many different businesses. Today, it is a gallery where painters, quilt makers and other artists display their work, and what better place to find Maureen Debenham's tearoom – a cosy and very pretty downstairs room where low beams, leaded windows, quarry tiled floor, traditional dark oak furniture and wreaths of dried flowers on the walls alongside the old prints of Guildford create a cosy, welcoming ambience.

If the weather is kind, there is more seating in a large courtyard that was once the stable yard, and the high old brick walls of other historic buildings and the tubs of plants and flowers set the scene for a peaceful and relaxing tea. Maureen's delicious cakes include carrot cake with lemon icing, fruit and date scones, and a very special cake that she created and named for artist John Russell's birthday – made with honey, figs, hazelnuts, apricots, butter and apples and served with set yoghurt and a sprinkling of nutmeg. *Teas served:* House Blend, Earl Grey, Assam, Darjeeling. *Herbal infusions are also offered.*

SHEPHERDS TEAROOMS

Owners: Yvonne and Richard Spence

35 Little London, Chichester
West Sussex PO19 2PL
Tel: 01243 774761

Directions
Little London is off East Street, one of the main shopping streets in Chichester.

Opening times
Open all year except Sundays.
Monday–Friday, 9.15 am–5 pm.
Saturday, 8 am–5 pm. Sunday, closed.

Awards
1989, 91, 93   Tea Council Award of Excellence
1990, 92, 95   Tea Council Top Tea Place of The Year
Egon Ronay recommended

Local Interest:
The medieval city walls, the Market Cross of 1501, the Cathedral, Chichester District Museum and the Guildhall are all within walking distance of Shepherds. Also nearby, the remains of a magnificent Roman Villa at Fishbourne to the south west of the city.

Housed in a fine Georgian listed building, Shepherds has a calm, friendly, living-room atmosphere and efficient, attentive waitresses. Floral curtains, ivory walls and rich red tablecloths covered with lace set a traditional theme and the room is decorated with plants and dried flowers and there are vases of fresh flowers on the tables. The windows of the conservatory at one end flood the room with light and warmth and make this a very popular, restful venue for tourists, local business people and weary shoppers who tuck into tasty rarebits, sandwiches and scrumptious sweet treats such as Earl Grey and Sultana Cake or Coffee and Walnut Sponge. The traditional cream tea with home-baked scones and generous portions of jam and cream are well worth a special visit.

Since 1987 when they acquired the tearooms, Yvonne and Richard Spence have constantly set very high standards and have researched different blends and suppliers of tea in order to offer only the best. Their special blends are so popular that they are now available by mail order or from the small shop. *Teas served:* English Breakfast, Ceylon Afternoon, Darjeeling, China Black, Earl Grey, Assam, Gunpowder, Jasmine. *Fruit flavoured teas and herbal infusions are also offered.*

A member of the Tea Council

The Tea Council

Guild of Tea Shops

E A S T
R E G I O N A L   M A P

THE STRAWBERRY TREE COUNTRY RESTAURANT

Owners: John and Wendy Bona

**Radwell Road, Milton Ernest
Bedford, Bedfordshire MK44 1RY
Tel: 01234 823633**

Directions
**Milton Ernest is just off the A6, three miles
north of Bedford.**

Opening times
Open February–end December except
Mondays and Tuesdays. Closed January.
Monday and Tuesday, closed. Wednesday–
Saturday, afternoon tea is served 3–5pm.

Award
Egon Ronay recommended

Local Interest:
*From the cottage, you can see the Old Hall, now a nursing
home, where Glenn Miller was billeted during the war. There
is also a very good Garden Centre in the village and lovely
surrounding countryside in which to walk. Bedford itself
has enjoyable walks along the river embankment and the
Bunyan Museum. John Bunyan joined an Independent
Church in Bedford in 1655 and became a popular preacher.
In prison after the Restoration, he wrote A Pilgrim's Progress.*

When you have finished exploring
Bedford, it is worth making the short
journey to Milton Ernest to find this
exquisitely pretty cottage with its
thatched roof, whitewashed walls and
leaded windows. The country restaurant
and tea shop are run very much as a caring family business and the atmosphere
inside, with open fireplaces, low beams
and pale pink walls, is as homely and
cosy as the outside is picturesque. The
three rooms are three hundred years old
and were once three separate cottages.
The name comes from the unusual
strawberry tree that Wendy and John

Bona found growing in the garden when
they bought the house 11 years ago.

Meringues are the speciality that
send customers into ecstasies. The
frothy, crispy shells are filled with lashings of cream and strawberries or chocolate, apple or brambles. Have one as part
of the set afternoon tea or try the cream
tea which comes with home-made
strawberry preserve and clotted cream.
No wonder the tea shop has been featured on Anglia Television's *Food Guide*!
Teas served: House Blend, Earl Grey,
Darjeeling, Assam, Ceylon. *Fruit infusion
is also offered.*

THE TEA ROOM

Owner: Barbara Johnson

**9 East Street, Kimbolton
Cambridgeshire PE18 0HJ
Tel: 01480 860415**

Directions
Kimbolton lies on the A45 between Cambridge and Northampton. The tea shop is at the east end of the village.

Opening times
Open all year except Mondays and mid-December—mid-January.
Monday, closed.
Tuesday—Saturday, 10 am–5.30 pm.
Sunday, 1.30–5.30 pm.

Award
Egon Ronay recommended

Local Interest:
Kimbolton Castle was built in the early 1600s and Catherine of Aragon, Henry VIII's first wife, lived the last 18 months of her life there after having been exiled by the King. The 15th century church is also worth a visit.

Barbara Johnson first thought of opening a tea shop in 1947 when she was personally trained by Lord Forte while working in a milk bar that he then owned in Brighton. The ambition surfaced again while very successfully running her house in Kimbolton as a Bed and Breakfast guest house and now visitors are stunned by the magic of the tearoom. For it is not just a house, it is a medieval hall with stone-tiled floors, wonderful low beams and a courtyard in York stone and with high old red brick walls covered with ivy and hanging flower baskets. The tearoom has just been enlarged to seat more eager customers and soon the garden will have the added charm of a fountain.

What could be more appropriate than to relax in the delightful garden or tearoom and tuck into one of Barbara's yummy cakes. There's a chocolate and raspberry roulade, a coffee chiffon cake with coffee cream and pecan nuts, or a light-as-air angel cake with strawberries, cream and raspberry sauce. Or you could indulge in a traditional cream tea or add a touch of summer luxury by adding fresh strawberries to the scones, jam and cream. *Teas served:* Earl Grey, Assam, Darjeeling, Lapsang Souchong, Coop 99 Tea. *Fruit flavoured teas are also offered.*

THE CAKE TABLE TEAROOM

Owners: Kathleen and Robert Albon

5 Fishmarket Street, Thaxted
Essex CM6 2PG
Tel: 01371 831206

Directions
Thaxted is well signposted on the B1051 and B184. The tearoom is tucked away to the left of the Guildhall.

Opening times
Open all year except Mondays during winter months, Christmas Day and Annual Holidays. Monday, 2–5 pm. Tuesday–Sunday, 11 am–5 pm. Open Bank Holidays.

Awards
1990   Tea Council Award of Excellence
1991   Tea Council Top Tea Place of The Year
1993–96   Egon Ronay recommended

Local Interest:
Thaxted Guildhall was built in 1390. The town is also famous for its medieval church and windmill.

One of Kathleen Albon's customers recently described her visit to The Cake Table as "just like being at home". The Albons have certainly achieved a very homely, old-fashioned atmosphere, with old beams, chintz curtains and furnishings, white china, an open fire, classical music and lots of really good home baking – coffee and walnut, traditional bread pudding and the scones being the most popular. The interior is so traditionally English and attractive that film crews have used the tea shop as the setting for television dramas and the stars have themselves stopped for tea.

Kathleen serves a very interesting range of well-known and more obscure teas from around the world. The menu gives valuable information about the taste and benefits of these and some, displayed on the dresser, are for sale. The shop also sells tea cosies, locally made hand-smocked aprons and floral prints by a local artist. In good weather, there is additional seating in the pretty walled garden where hanging baskets continue the theme of old world charm. *Teas served:* House Blend, Assam, Darjeeling, Earl Grey, English Breakfast, Keemun, Kenya, Lapsang Souchong, Yunnan, Russian Caravan, Oolong, Gunpowder, Japanese Sencha, Lychee, Decaffeinated, Organic, iced tea on summer days. *Fruit flavoured teas and herbal infusions are also offered.*

THE CROOKED COTTAGE TEA ROOMS

Owner: Anne Woolfson

**1 The Quay, Burnham-on-Crouch
Essex CM0 8AS
Tel: 01621 783868
Fax: 01621 783868**

Directions
**There is pedestrian access only. Walk down
the High Street until you see, on the right, a**
restaurant called Simply Red. A pathway to
the sides leads to the Tea Rooms. There is also
access from the river front.

Opening times
Open March–October and weekends only
1st November–1st March.
Monday, closed except Bank Holidays.
Tuesday–Sunday, 10 am–6 pm. 🚭

Local Interest:
*The quaint little sailing town has a marina, a clock tower,
fresh shellfish stalls by the war memorial and wonderful
walks along the waterside.*

This very crooked cottage is over 300 years old and was once a fisherman's home. There are boatyards on either side and a dock and the tearoom has a wonderful view over a picturesque stretch of the river with its steady stream of fishing boats and yachts. The outside of the interesting little house is covered with white weatherboards and the inside of the oak-beamed room is filled with ornaments and decorative objects and lots and lots of pictures of cats, for the owner of the tearoom, Anne Woolfson is a dedicated cat-lover.

In summer there are ten tables in the charming secluded cottage garden where a pond with fish, a rockery, a sundial, old-fashioned roses and lots of colourful flowers blend all the elements of the perfect traditional English garden. There is an excellent selection of traditional goodies on the menu, too, and with one of 18 different teas, you can enjoy scones, cinnamon toast, marmite soldiers, gingerbread men and luscious cakes that include hot Devon Apple Cake covered with cream. On sale also is a range of the famous locally-made Burnham mustard, mustard pots, jams and a speciality salad dressing called Burnham Mud! *Teas served:* Ceylon, Assam, Kenya, Darjeeling, Earl Grey, China Jasmine. *Fruit flavoured and herbal teas are also offered.*

THE TEA ROOM

Manageress: Colette Harrington

**Wilkin & Sons Ltd
Tiptree, Essex CO5 0RF
Tel: 01621 815407   Fax: 01621 819468**

For group bookings, please telephone
Angela Marris on 01621 815407.

Directions
**Leave the A12 at Kelvedon and take the B1023
to Tiptree (4 miles). Cross the B1022 into
Tiptree Village heading for Tollesbury. As you**
leave the village, Wilkin & Sons is immediately
on the right. The entrance to the tea room is 200
metres further on, on the right, well signposted.
If lost ask for 'the jam factory'.

Opening times
June–late August, open 7 days a week,
10 am–5 pm. End of August–end of May, open
Monday–Saturday, 10 am–5 pm. Closed Sunday.

Local Interest:
*Close by, there are Pick-Your-Own fruit farms, the River
Blackwater for fishing and sailing, the riverside town of
Maldon, Chappel steam railway museum, Layer Marney
Towers (a historic house), Colchester, the oldest recorded town
in Britain, Colchester zoo, and various parks and gardens.*

Wilkin & Sons Tiptree Tea Room is located in an old building on their fruit farm, right next door to the famous jam factory. Manageress, Colette Harrington offers a range of quality sandwiches, and home-made scones and cakes, such as Lemon Meringue Pie and walnut cake. The speciality is the cream tea served with Tiptree's delicious and daintily-named 'Little Scarlet' preserve and a pot of Tiptree tea.

The tea room seats 60 and welcomes coach parties and special visits for birthday teas and anniversaries. There is the added attraction of the Jam Shop and Museum in the same group of buildings as the tea room, so visitors can go home with a ready supply of jams and teas – both loose and in bags – for tea-times at home. *Teas served:* Assam, Darjeeling, Ceylon, Earl Grey.

CASTLE TEAROOM

Owner: Janet Tucker

**14 Castle Street
Berkhamsted
Hertfordshire HP4 2BQ
Tel: 01442 866974**

Directions

**In Berkhamsted, opposite St Peter's
Churchyard, follow signs to the Castle. One
hundred yards from Castle Street, you will see
a black teapot sign, indicating the tearoom.**

Opening times
Open all year except Mondays, Christmas
Day and Boxing Day. Tuesday–Saturday,
10 am–5.30 pm. Sundays, 12 noon–5.30 pm.
Bank Holidays, 12 noon–6 pm. 🚭

Award
Egon Ronay recommended

Local Interest:
*The ruins of the castle make an interesting walk. It was here
that William the Conqueror accepted the Saxon surrender
in 1066 and the Black Prince honeymooned in the 14th
century. Also in the town is a 13th century church and
Berkhamsted School, the public school for boys, which dates
back to 1544. Nearby Chiltern countryside and the banks of
the canal are also good for walking.*

The Castle tearoom is on the ground floor of a listed 1844 building in the conservation area of Berkhamsted, very close to the castle and 16th century courthouse. Janet Tucker has created an extremely friendly, Edwardian-style tea shop where customers feel as comfortable as in their own living room and where there are daily newspapers, magazines and table puzzles to amuse the children. The lace-covered tables are laid with pretty willow pattern china and decorated with fresh flowers, the home-baked cakes and scones are a treat and every customer is looked after with great care and attention.

Visitors come from all over the world, including Romania and Russia, and the residents of Neuisenburg near Frankfurt in Germany also had the chance to enjoy British tea-time traditions and sample the Castle Tearoom's specialities when Janet took her china, cakes, scones and clotted cream there as part of a weekend of exchange activities between the twinned towns in 1992. The tearoom was set up in Neuisenburg's Town Hall and served a constant stream of local visitors who were thrilled to sample such scrumptious British food. *Teas served:* 20 different teas including Traditional English, English Breakfast, Earl Grey, Darjeeling, Assam, Decaffeinated. *Herbal infusions are also offered.*

THE TEA & COFFEE HOUSE

Owner: Shirley Davies

6A Arcade Walk
Hitchin, Herts SG5 1EE
Tel: 01462 433631

Directions
The shop is just off the High Street in the old arcade.

Opening times
Open all year except Sunday.
Monday, Tuesday, Thursday, Friday,
9.30 am–5 pm. Wednesday, 9.30 am–4.30 pm.
Saturday, 9 am–5 pm. 🚭

Local Interest:
Hitchin Museum houses a Victorian chemist shop and all the local history, and near the shop are the very pretty Civic Gardens.

The Tea & Coffee House is a small privately owned business that started as a shop selling specialist teas and coffees in 1986 and which moved to bigger premises in 1993 when the seating area was created alongside. The range of teas offers an almost unique opportunity for customers to sample and buy really unusual blends and speciality teas and coffees.

The food is of as high a quality as the beverages, and Shirley is sometimes asked by her customers whether they should photograph or eat the open sandwiches – they are so beautiful and impressive. Favourite cakes include chocolate fudge cake, coffee cake and banana and raisin cake.

The shop's staff are extremely helpful with advice about which tea to order and, when you have found one you like, you can buy more from the counter to take home or give as a gift. The teas are all stored in old-fashioned Chinese style black, burgundy and gold caddies and their colours set the theme for the shop. *Teas served:* 70 different varieties including a House Blend (Assam & Kenya), Darjeeling, Assam, Ceylon, Kenya, China Silver Tip Oolong, Ceylon, African, China, Japanese, exotic flavoured teas. *Fruit flavoured tea and herbal infusions are also available.*

MARGARET'S TEA ROOMS

Owner: Margaret Bacon

**Chestnut Farmhouse, The Street
Baconsthorpe, Near Holt, Norfolk
NR25 6AB
Tel: 01263 577614**

Directions
Baconsthorpe lies 3 miles south of the A148,
the Holt by-pass. Follow the road south

and Margaret's is about 400 yards from the
Holt–Norwich (B1149) roundabout.

Opening times
Open from the beginning of March to the end
of October. Mondays, closed except Bank
Holidays and in July and August.
Tuesday–Sunday, 10.30 am–5.30 pm.

Local Interest:
*The ruins of Baconsthorpe Castle are less than 5 minutes'
walk away and a short drive takes you to Cromer and the
north Norfolk coast with its beaches and bays. The area is
very popular with bird-watchers. Nearby Holt is an extremely
interesting Georgian town with very attractive shops.*

Margaret Bacon's mid-17th century farmhouse is a warm, welcoming, homely guest house and her garden and two parlours – the Harebell and the Strawberry parlour – all offer very pretty, traditional settings for a perfect afternoon tea. Lace tablecloths set off the themed china used in the two rooms and you really feel as if you are visiting someone in their own home. In the colder months, an oak fire in the Strawberry parlour and a wood burning stove in the Harebell add to the comfortable warmth.

Margaret's home cooking makes every meal special. She makes all the breads, cakes, biscuits, scones, soups, jams, pickles herself in the farmhouse kitchen and the menu offers healthy alternatives for those who worry a little about their diet and cholesterol levels. But for those who want to indulge, there are delicious pies and quiches, scones with jam and cream, carrot cakes, coffee and walnut, bakewell tart, hot marmalade bread pudding with cream, and apricot shortbread.

While Margaret is busy cooking and serving tea, her husband, Roger, makes solid wood furniture in his workshop at the back of the house and there are photographs and samples of his work in the house. *Teas served:* Darjeeling, Assam, Ceylon, Lapsang Souchong, Earl Grey. *A few herbal infusions are also available.*

THE SWAN

Owner: Michael R. Grange

High Street
Lavenham
Sudbury, Suffolk
CO10 9QA
Tel: 01787 247477
Fax: 01787 248286

Directions
Lavenham is on the B1141 between Ipswich and Bury St Edmunds. The Swan is in the centre of the town.

Opening times
The Swan Hotel is open all year.
Tea is served in the lounge from 3–5.30 pm.

Local Interest:
In the Middle ages, Lavenham was the centre of the wool trade and one of the wealthiest towns in England. Walk from The Swan to the medieval Guildhall (National Trust), the Priory, the Little Hall and the cathedral-like Church of St Peter and St Paul.

In the 15th century, four timbered houses in the centre of this incredibly unspoilt and picturesque town were united to form the Swan Hotel and today it is still a hotel of great character and charm and a perfectly wonderful place to stop for a traditional English tea. The cosy, comfortable lounge has quaint snug corners that are ideal for a quiet, refined cup of tea, open fireplaces where roaring log fires crackle their welcome in winter months, generous arrangements of fresh and dried flowers all over the room and a lovely view of the walled, cloistered garden with its lawn surrounded by pretty borders. In summer, customers spill out into this beautiful space for their three course tea that is served on silver, tiered cake stands, or a cream tea with home-baked scones, home-made jams and Cornish clotted cream.

At weekends, the old-world atmosphere of refinement and gentle pleasure is enhanced by harpsichord recitals. You will feel as if you have settled into a genteel country house where afternoon refreshment is an essential part of each day's enjoyment. *Teas served:* House Blend, Earl Grey, Assam, Darjeeling, Lapsang Souchong.

MIDLANDS
REGIONAL MAP

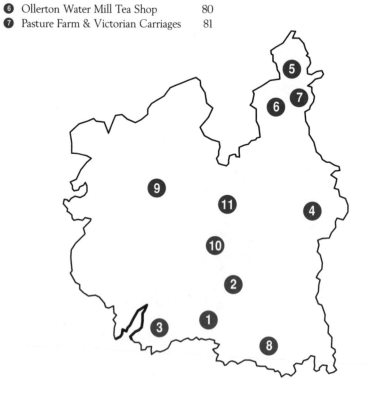

Bo-PEEP TEAROOMS

Owners: Bob and Judy Hiscoke

**Riverside, Bourton-on-the-Water
Cheltenham, Gloucestershire
GL54 2DP
Tel: 01451 822005**

Directions
**Bourton-on-the-Water is situated just off the
A429 between Stow-on-the-Wold and Cirencester. Park in the main car park, cross the
High Street and turn right. The footbridge**
adjacent to the road bridge takes you over the
river and directly to the tearooms.

Opening times
Open all year. Monday–Sunday in winter,
10.30 am–5 pm. In summer, 10.30 am–6 pm.
During school holidays and peak times,
10.30 am–8 pm.

Awards
1992, 93 & 94 Tea Council Award of Excellence
Egon Ronay recommended

Local Interest:
*There is a model of the village in the garden of The New
Inn, a model railway, an exhibition of perfumerie,
Birdland (a collection of 600 different species of birds)
and a motor museum.*

What could be a more perfect setting
for tea than a garden seat beside the River
Windrush as it flows gently through the
middle of this very pretty Cotswold
village, under elegant low stone 18th century bridges and alongside immaculate
gardens with their neat lawns and colourful flower borders. Part of Bob and Judy
Hiscoke's home dates from the 17th
century and the period feel is heightened
by the old Cotswold stone walling and,
in the tearoom itself, antique wood
panelling from Elmley Castle.

The list of teas offers a comprehensive range, including, unusually, Japanese
Sencha – a green tea with a pale liquor
and a fresh, flowery taste. To help less
experienced tea drinkers, the menu very
thoughtfully indicates the strength of
the different teas with a rating scale
from 1 to 8.

The menu also tempts you with all
sorts of rich and delicious cakes, and the
huge home-made scones are served with
Cornish clotted cream and lashings of
local jam. *Teas served:* House Blend, English Breakfast, Earl Grey, Darjeeling,
Assam, Nilgiri, Lapsang Souchong,
Oolong, Jasmine, Gunpowder, Keemun,
Rose Petal, Ceylon, Kenya, Russian,
Japanese Sencha. *Fruit flavoured and
herbal teas are also offered.*

THE MARSHMALLOW

Owner: Valerie West

**High Street, Moreton-in-Marsh
Gloucestershire GL56 0AT
Tel: 01608 651536**

Directions
Moreton-in-Marsh is on the A429 between Stratford-upon-Avon and Stow-on-the-Wold. The tea shop is at the north end of the town, in the main shopping street, not far from the station.

Opening times
Open all year.
Monday, 10 am–5 pm. Tuesday, 10 am–4 pm.
Wednesday–Saturday, 10 am–9.30 pm.
Sunday, 10.30 am–9.30 pm.

Local Interest:
The High Street in which the Marshmallow stands was part of the Roman Fosse Way that ran from Devon to the north east of England. All around the town there are examples of typical Cotswold houses with their steeply pitched roofs. Also, lots of antique shops and the Wellington Art Gallery for those interested in paintings of aircraft.

Having never been involved in catering before acquiring this lovely Grade II listed building, Valerie West now runs a thriving restaurant and tearoom right in the heart of the busy town that was once very important in the wool trade. Within ten days of moving in, Valerie had rebuilt and opened her 96 seat dining room and is busy all year with tourists, regular customers and passing visitors, particularly on Tuesdays when the traders' market comes to town.

The front of the building is covered with Virginia Creeper and in the flagstoned courtyard at the back, where there are more tables, hanging flower baskets and more greenery create a very restful place in which to sit and have tea. Waitresses are dressed in gentle shades of peach and pale green, furnishings are pine, set against original stone walls, and there is a view through to the homely kitchen where copper pots and pans decorate the walls and the chefs create wonderful cakes and savouries. The cake trolley is laden with truly delicious creations – chocolate mousses, roulades, mille feuille gâteaux, pecan Danish pastries and so much more to tempt you. *Teas served:* House Blend, Earl Grey, Assam, Lapsang Souchong, Darjeeling, Traditional. *Fruit flavoured and herbal teas are also offered.*

TETBURY GALLERY TEAROOM

Owners: Jane Maile and
Helen Joyner

**18 Market Place, Tetbury
Gloucestershire GL8 8DD
Tel: 01666 503412**

Directions
Tetbury is ten miles from Junction 17 on the
M4 and ten miles from Cirencester. The
Gallery Tearoom is situated in the centre of town, just along the road, on the opposite side, to the pillared Market House.

Opening times
Open 7 days a week all year except
2 weeks in mid-December.
Times vary according to season. 🚭

Local Interest:
Walk from the tea shop to the 1655 Market House, the Georgian Parish Church of St Mary the Virgin with a spire that is the fourth highest in England. Chipping Steps was, for centuries, the sight of 'Mop Fairs' where labourers, shepherds and domestic staff sought employment, and Gunstool Hill is said to have been the sight of a ducking stool and is today the venue for the weekly livestock market.

Tourist guides to the Cotswolds almost run out of superlatives in writing about Tetbury. It is described as a "Cotswold gem", a "superb touring centre", a "most delightful shopping centre" and it is said to have "some of the handsomest rows of houses in the Cotswolds" and to retain "the authentic harmony of a 17th century wool town".

The very centre of town offers a tranquil atmosphere, ancient street names and elegant Georgian façades. Behind one of these, in what was originally the drawing room of an 18th century house, is a tearoom where linen tablecloths, fine bone china and walls hung with fine art combine to recall a more leisurely bygone era. If the weather is fine, there is more seating in a pretty walled courtyard and here you can relax and enjoy some of Jane Maile and Helen Joyner's traditional English home baking. Their cakes and scones are so good that they have been urged to publish a book of recipes, something they are now seriously planning to do. *Teas served:* Breakfast Blend, Earl Grey, Darjeeling, Assam, Ceylon, Lapsang Souchong. *Fruit flavoured and herbal teas are also offered.*

ELEANOR HOUSE TEASHOP & RESTAURANT

Owners: Roger and Victoria Newman

**Geddington, Northamptonshire
NN14 1AD
Tel: 01536 742266   Fax: 01536 742266**

Directions
Geddington is on the A43 between Kettering and Corby. The tea shop is in the centre of the village, opposite Eleanor Cross.

Opening times
June–September, Monday, closed.
Tuesday–Saturday, 11.30 am–5.30 pm.
Sunday, 11.30 am–6 pm.
October–May, open every Sunday
and Bank Holidays.
The restaurant is open all year for bookings.

Local Interest:
The 13th century Eleanor Cross is the finest example of only three remaining crosses of this type. Nearby, Boughton House, the home of the Duke of Buccleuch, is known as the English Versailles and is open to the public in August (the grounds are open from April–October). Nottinghamshire is known as a county of Squires and Spires and not far away, there are many fine castles, houses, churches, parks and forests to visit.

Taking tea in Eleanor House is like visiting good friends in their living room. There is a view through to the kitchen where all the wonderful cakes are baked every day, the furnishings are all old pine, and on the colour-washed walls hang paintings and drawings by local artists. High shelves display an attractive collection of strange teapots, colourful plates, pretty jam pots and other tewares, and the cakes are displayed on traditional glass stands.

Gentle classical music in the background creates a calm, unhurried atmosphere and you can sit back and indulge in a delicious sandwich, freshly baked scones or a cake selected from the hand-written menu.

Choose from rich chocolate marzipan cake, fresh lime and coconut cake, rich own recipe tea-cakes with apricots, or choux buns filled with clotted cream and topped with coffee icing and flaked almonds. The pretty teapots are regularly topped up without you having to ask, and nothing is too much trouble for the owners, Roger and Victoria Newman, who will serve you an exceptionally good tea. *Teas served:* Assam, Ceylon, Darjeeling, Earl Grey, Keemun, Lapsang Souchong, Decaffeinated Ceylon and Earl Grey. *Fruit flavoured and herbal teas are also offered.*

OLDE SCHOOL TEAROOM

Owner: Gwen Elliott

**Carburton, Near Worksop
Nottinghamshire S80 3BP
Tel: 01909 483517**

Directions
**Carburton is on the B6034 that runs from
Worksop to Allerton. The Olde School
Tearoom is at the crossroads with the road that
runs from Clumber Park to Norton village.**

Opening times
Open all year except January and Mondays.
Monday, closed.
Tuesday–Friday, 10 am–4.30 pm.
Saturday and Sunday, 10 am–5 pm.

Award
1992   Tea Council Award of Excellence

Local Interest:
*The Olde School is opposite one of the entrances to
Clumber Park and as Carburton is in the middle of
Sherwood Forest it is an excellent area for walks. At
nearby Edwinstow is the Sherwood Forest Visitor Centre
and at Newark, an interesting castle.*

Many of the regular customers in this converted 1930s school are local people who love the peace and quiet of a country tearoom. But it is also an ideal place for tourists after a drive or ramble in Sherwood Forest or Clumber Park. Gwen Elliott has preserved the spirit of the school building and has an old school desk in the entrance, her menu written up on the blackboard and easel and the original children's hand basins in the wash rooms. The old school shelves, once used for reference books and stacks of homework, now display woodwork, greetings cards and handmade prints by local artists. The partition that in the past divided the main classroom into two is now used to make a separate room for private parties, and the old school bell is still available to attract the attention of large groups if they are being too jolly and making too much noise!

Good service and value are important to Gwen and her menu offers a very reasonably priced selection of home-made savouries and cakes and fresh cut sandwiches. The most popular cake is something her mother used to make when Gwen was a child – a fruit slice with a pastry base, a layer of jam and topping of sponge full of dried fruits. *Teas served:* House Blend, Assam, Darjeeling, Earl Grey, Ceylon.

OLLERTON WATER MILL TEA SHOP

Owners: Kate and Ellen Mettam

**Ollerton Mill, Market Place
Ollerton, Newark
Nottinghamshire NG22 9AA
Tel: 01623 824094/822469**

Directions
Ollerton lies at the junction of the A614 and B616, between Worksop and Nottingham. The Water Mill and Tea Shop are in the centre of the village, almost opposite the church.

Opening times
Open April–October, Wednesday–Sunday, 10.30 am–5 pm. Open every Bank Holiday and any other time by arrangement.

Award
1994   Tea Council Award of Excellence

Local Interest:
The mill has an exhibition with colourful display panels which tell the story of the mill. There is also a video which shows the mill grinding and producing flour.

Ollerton is situated on the edge of Sherwood Forest in a corner of rural England that has remained unchanged for three hundred years, and the Mill stands on the same spot as the medieval mill that is mentioned in the Doomsday Book. Since 1921, it has been in the Mettam family who have been millers for many generations and whose family tree has been traced back to 1635. In 1993, it was lovingly restored by them and now Kate and Ellen's husbands manage the mill while they and their four daughters run the tea shop which is housed in the Old Millwright's workshop. The entrance has a wonderful view of the water wheel and mill race and the tea shop itself looks directly over the River Maun.

This is a really delightful spot and visitors have the chance to learn a little about what life was like for a working miller in the 18th century at the same time as enjoying a really special afternoon tea in the old-fashioned style. All the cakes are baked on the premises with flour that is ground and sold in the mill. Tuck into chocolate fudge or date and walnut or go for the Ollerton Mill Cream Tea which is perfect, with three dainty fruit or plain scones served with jam and cream. *Teas served:* House Blend, Earl Grey, English Breakfast. *Fruit and herbal infusions are also offered.*

PASTURE FARM & VICTORIAN CARRIAGES

Owners: Helen & Mark Evans

**Pasture Farm, Main Street
Kirton, Newark
Nottinghamshire NG22 9LP
Tel: 01623 836291**

Directions

Kirton is 3½ miles from the A1 and the A614, mid-way between Ollerton and Tuxford on the A6075 Mansfield to Lincoln road. Pasture Farm is in the centre of the village, 75 yards from the church, almost opposite the Fox pub.

Opening times

Open April–September inclusive. Monday, closed. Tuesday–Sunday, 11 am–5 pm. October–March, only open Saturday and Sunday. Closed February.

Local Interest:

Pasture Farm has a Working Horse Drawn Carriage Driving Centre, stables and Museum. You can take lessons in carriage driving or arrange a two day tour in a Landau drawn by a pair of carriage horses. Travel in style along the ancient Great North Road and quiet country by-ways, visiting friendly country inns along the way.

Pasture Farm, a traditional Nottinghamshire farmhouse, dates back to about 1800 and has retained a great deal of its original character, so it is immediately apparent why Mark and Helen Evans chose it as the venue for their dream tea room. With its original exposed oak beamed ceiling, spacious rooms, hall ways, tall chimneys and delightful grounds, it is the perfect location in which to recreate the traditional teas of last century.

Personal service, home cooking and value for money are the key words at Pasture Farm. Everything is freshly prepared in the farmhouse kitchen and lunches, Cream Teas and Afternoon Teas are served on Royal Doulton Old Country Rose fine bone china.

The Victorian atmosphere of Pasture Farm is heightened by the wonderful array of horse-drawn carriages in the museum. There are harnesses and whips and other working carriage memorabilia, there are liveried coachmen, a groom, the horses he cares for and sometimes a farrier. If you would like to enjoy a ride that captures the spirit of the past, you can dress up in Victorian period costumes and be carried away in the Wagonette or an original Landau before returning to the farm for a traditional tea. *Teas served:* House Blend, Earl Grey, Darjeeling, Fine Assam, other speciality teas.

ANNIE'S TEA ROOMS

Owner: Jean Ann Rowlands

79 High Street, Wallingford
Oxfordshire OX10 0BX
Tel: 01491 836308

Directions
Wallingford is situated at the junction of the A329, Reading to Oxford road, and the A4130, Henley to Wantage road. Annie's is in the High Street, just along from the crossroads with St Martin's Street and Castle Street.

Opening times
Open all year except Bank Holidays.
Monday, Tuesday, Thursday–Saturday,
10 am–5 pm (5.30 pm in July,
August and September).
Sunday (open only in July, August
and September), 2.30–5.30 pm.
Wednesday, closed.

Local Interest:
The Castle grounds are excellent for walks and hold concerts on summer Sundays. There is a regatta in May, a carnival in June and a Victorian celebration in December when the entire town participates in entertainments and markets.

Wallingford's history goes back to the granting of its charter in 1155 and it has links with a number of interesting personalities from the past, including Oliver Cromwell. The ruins of the largest castle in England stand round the corner from Annie's and stones from here were included in the building of Windsor Castle.

Right in the centre of town, in a Grade II listed building that is over 300 years old, Jean Ann Rowlands gives a very warm welcome to visitors from all over the world who come to taste her wonderful home-baked cakes, scones, teacakes, pies and jams. Jean's speciality is her own original Cinnamon-flavoured

Wallingford Muffin which has a warm soft apple mixture in the middle that oozes out when you open it up.

The pretty pink and burgundy room is a relaxing setting to enjoy your tea. The walls are decorated with old paintings and views of Wallingford and paintings by local customers are displayed for sale. On fine days, a small, walled cottage garden at the back allows alfresco teas after you have explored the ancient highways and byways of the town. *Teas served:* Indian, Earl Grey, Ceylon, Darjeeling, Traditional English Blend, Assam, Lapsang Souchong. *Fruit flavoured and herbal teas are also offered.*

SIX ASHES TEAROOM & RESTAURANT

Owners: Jenny and Geoff Blore

Six Ashes, Near Bridgnorth
Shropshire WV15 6EN
Tel: 01384 221216

Directions
Six Ashes Tearoom is situated on the A458, six

and a half miles from Bridgnorth and eight miles from Stourbridge.

Opening times
Open all year except Mondays and Tuesdays.
Monday and Tuesday, closed.
Wednesday–Friday, 11 am–4.30 pm.
Saturday and Sunday, 10 am–5 pm.

Local Interest:
Nearby Stockbridge has glass factories open to the public and near the very pretty town of Bridgnorth is a motor museum. The countryside round about is wonderful for walking.

Regular customers to Six Ashes Tearoom think nothing of travelling 60 miles a week in order to relish the delicious, thoughtfully prepared specialities that Jenny Blore creates for the attractive, comfortable tea shop that she owns and runs with her husband, Geoff.

The menu is devised around carefully selected products, lays the emphasis on healthy eating and offers an excellent range of low fat recipes, vegetarian dishes and wonderful home-baked treats. Soups are made with fresh vegetables and herbs, pastries use only vegetable fat, all eggs are free range and the counter always displays at least 14 fabulous home-made cakes, trifles and gateaux.

Jenny and Geoff have put an enormous amount of care and attention into arranging everything to ensure that all visitors have a truly enjoyable time here. After requests by lots of regulars, the Blores now open in the evenings. They have top quality chefs creating wonderful food and the standard is so high and the reputation spreading so fast that all the tables are already booked for evenings weeks ahead. And a very warm welcome means that you will always enjoy your meal, whether it's tea or dinner. *Teas served:* House Blend, English Breakfast, Earl Grey, Ceylon, Darjeeling, Assam, Rooibosch. *Herbal teas are also offered.*

BENSON'S OF STRATFORD-UPON-AVON

Owner: Max Lawrence

**4 Bards Walk, Stratford-upon-Avon
Warwickshire CU37 6EY
Tel: 01789 261116**

Directions

Benson's is off Henley Street, two minutes walk from Shakespeare's birthplace in the town centre.

Opening times

Open all year except Sundays in winter.
Monday–Friday, 10 am–5.30 pm.
Saturday, 8.30 am–5.30 pm.
Sunday (summer only), 10 am-4.30 pm.

Local Interest:

Benson's is right in the centre of Shakespeare's town. From the shop you can easily walk to Shakespeare's birthplace, his daughter, Judith's home and Holy Trinity Church where he is buried. Also close by is Harvard House, home of the man who set up Harvard University in the USA and a place of pilgrimage for Americans.

This very light and airy conservatory-style tea shop is in a refurbished Victorian arcade that was once Osbornes Court, a row of eight little cottages converted from a Malt House between 1809 and 1821. The display of the patisseries that fills the 19th century window of the shop will tempt you inside and you will find yourself in an extremely calm and relaxing interior that is bright with the colour of the plants and flowers around the room and the original watercolours on the walls.

Max Lawrence worked in Switzerland for a while and has a flair for serving mouthwatering pastries. The mille feuille with fresh fruit is too good to miss but if you prefer something savoury with your afternoon tea, the gourmet sandwiches with all sorts of possible fillings are absolutely wonderful. Try carved ham with cream cheese and melon or Stilton with apple, or make up your own combination. A set afternoon tea will give you smoked salmon sandwiches followed by home-baked scones with jam and cream and a speciality tea served in one of the Shakespeare teapots, each of which represents a different Shakespeare play. *Teas served:* House Blend, Earl Grey, English Breakfast, Assam, Darjeeling, Ceylon, Decaffeinated, Lapsang Souchong. *Herbal teas are also offered.*

TIME FOR TEA

Owner: Helena Shaw

**40 Castle Hill
Kenilworth
Warwickshire CV8 1NB
Tel: 01926 512675**

Directions
**Approach Kenilworth on the A452,
Birmingham to Leamington Spa route.
This becomes the B4103 which leads
directly to Kenilworth Castle. Turn left into
Castle Green and left again into Castle Hill.
Time For Tea is next to the castle and opposite
Abbey Fields.**

Opening times
**Open all year except Mondays. Monday, closed.
Tuesday–Sunday, 10.30 am–5 pm
(10.30 am–5 pm November–March).**

Local Interest:
*Visit Kenilworth Castle and enjoy walks in Abbey Fields
around the ruins of the Abbey and on a variety of footpaths
that start near the tea shop. The streets of the town are also
very interesting and have quaint old shops.*

Helena Shaw actually made up her mind to open her own tea shop while sitting round a table with various friends in a Darjeeling Guest House. She had been toying with the idea for some time and the situation and the encouragement of the others pushed her into vowing to do it as soon as she got back to England. Now, she is very firmly established in this lovely Grade II listed building in one of Kenilworth's prettiest streets, running an incredibly successful tea shop that everyone absolutely loves. It has very quickly become a regular haunt for locals who love the friendly, helpful, chatty atmosphere and a haven for tourists who have made such comments in the visitors' book as "Brilliant – the best tea shop in the world," and "Excellent. We'll be back!"

The charm of the two pine-furnished rooms is enhanced by a collection of pretty teapots and tea caddies that Helena has collected since she was 14 years old. Tuck into wonderful fig and walnut, honey and coconut, and chocolate orange cake. You cannot fail to enjoy yourself. *Teas served:* Earl Grey, Assam, Darjeeling, Ceylon, Lapsang Souchong, Traditional English, Jasmine. *Herbal infusions are also offered.*

NORTH EAST
REGIONAL MAP

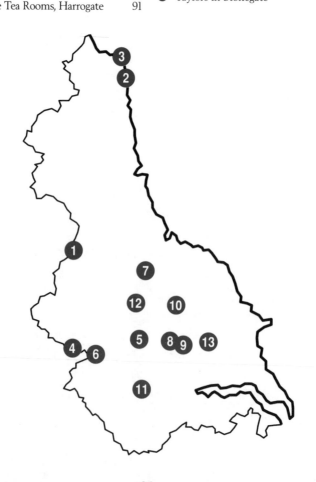

THE MARKET PLACE TEASHOP

Owner: Robert Hilton

**29 Market Place, Barnard Castle
County Durham DL12 8NE
Tel: 01833 690110**

Directions
The tea shop is in the centre of the cobbled Market Place.

Opening times
Open all year except two weeks at Christmas.
Monday–Saturday, 10 am–5.30 pm.
Sunday, 3–5.30 pm.

Awards
Egon Ronay recommended

Local Interest:
The town has interesting antique and craft shops in which to browse. On the outskirts, visit the Bowes Museum which has one of the finest art collections outside London, and Raby Castle, the seat of Lord Barnard. Drive to nearby High Force, the highest waterfall in England, and enjoy surrounding Teesdale countryside.

In the very heart of this attractive old market town, you will find the Market Place Teashop in an early 17th century building that long ago was a house before it became a pub and later a gentleman's outfitters selling typical country garments to local farm workers. The front of the tea shop was probably the original master's house, and servants quarters and stables were behind and alongside in Waterloo Yard. Today, the upstairs Artisan shop and picture gallery has a good selection of gifts, fabrics, prints and original paintings.

The tea shop itself is a charming room full of character, with flagstones on the floor and an open stone fireplace. Tea is served in silver teapots by friendly waitresses in smart burgundy-striped uniforms and they will bring you whatever you choose from the tempting list of home-baked cakes that changes daily. Try the meringues filled with cream and strawberries, the strawberry tarts or the Yorkshire Curd Cheesecake. The high quality of all the food and the attractive, welcoming atmosphere make this an excellent place for lunch or afternoon tea. *Teas served:* Typhoo, Earl Grey, Ceylon, Traditional English, Assam, Darjeeling, Lapsang Souchong, China. *Fruit flavoured and herbal teas are also offered.*

THE TEA COSY TEA ROOM

Owners: Sheila and Wyn Porteous

23 Northumberland Street
Alnmouth
Northumberland NE66 2RJ
Tel: 01665 830393

Directions
Take the A1068 northbound from Warkworth,
southbound from Alnwick. Turn right onto the

B1339 at a roundabout to Alnmouth which is approximately 1 mile along this road.

Opening times
In summer, open 7 days a week,
10 am–5.30 pm.
In winter, open Tuesday–Sunday,
11 am–4 pm.
Monday closed.

Local Interest:
Alnmouth itself is an interesting and picturesque village. Also, the second oldest golf course in Britain, lovely beaches, walking and fishing.

The aptly named Tea Cosy is a tea room by day and a bistro by night and whatever time you choose to visit, you will always find a really warm welcome and friendly atmosphere. The shop sits very happily in a pretty double fronted 270-year-old building and is full of character. The walls are decorated with fascinating old prints of old Alnmouth and local personalities, and the real focal point is the incredible old stone fireplace with cast iron oven that Wyn and Sheila discovered when they were doing some basic renovation work.

The Porteous's original idea was to run a village store here with a few tables, but the early success of the small tea room led them to expand that side of the business and close down the store. Their menu is packed with local traditionals such as Northumbrian Stottie – a sort of round, flat bread – and Singing Hinnies – fruited flat griddle cakes served with butter and strawberry jam. And all the old favourites are there too – toasted muffins, hot buttered crumpets, buttery tea cakes, coffee and walnut cakes, chocolate and apple cake and apple pie. If you are up in this part of the world, don't miss this lovely shop. *Teas served:* House Blend (specially blended to suit the local water), Assam, Darjeeling, Earl Grey, Lemon. *Herbal and fruit infusions are also offered.*

THE COPPER KETTLE TEA ROOMS

Owners: Rosemary Christie and David Bates

21 Front Street, Bamburgh
Northumbria NE69 7BW
Tel: 01668 214315

Directions
Turn off the A1 towards the coast on either the B1341 or the B1342. Both roads lead to Bamburgh and the tearoom is situated in the heart of the village.

Opening times
Monday–Friday, March, April, October, 10.30 am–5 pm; May–September, 10.30 am–5.30 pm. Saturday & Sunday, March–October, 10.30 am–5.30 pm. Closed, November–end February. Open some weekends in November and December.

Local Interest:
Visit the Norman Castle and the 13th century church where you will find the grave of Grace Darling, the heroine of the rescue of survivors from a wrecked steamer. The Grace Darling Museum houses more souvenirs.

A bright display of colourful flowers outside the front door and windows welcomes you to this delightful 18th century cottage tearoom. After a tour of Bamburgh's Norman Castle or a walk in the sea air, you simply must not miss afternoon tea in the old-fashioned charm of the house or cottage garden. With the exception of the bread and teacakes, everything on the tempting menu is baked on the premises and the selection is mouthwatering – gingerbread, coffee walnut cake, cherry madeira, scotch pancakes with maple syrup, and chocolate caramel shortbread, flapjacks and scones.

There is also an incredibly wide range of teas and infusions and if you want to take home more of the one you enjoyed with your tea, the gift shop offers everything from a single teabag to boxes and gift packs. And how will you be able to resist the Belgian chocolates, quality preserves, sweets and biscuits that are also displayed on the shelves?

Teas served: Assam, Ceylon, China, Darjeeling, Earl Grey, English Breakfast, Lapsang Souchong, Orange Pekoe, Rose Pouchong, Decaffeinated, Organic. *Fruit flavoured and herbal teas are also offered.*

BARDEN TOWER TEAROOMS

Owners: Robert Hodgson and
Jo Parkinson

**Barden, Near Skipton
North Yorkshire BD23 6AS
Tel: 01756 720616**

Directions
From Leeds, take the A65 to Addingham. Follow directions to Bolton Abbey. Take the B6160 to Burnsall. Barden is between Bolton Abbey and Burnsall, approximately 3 miles from Bolton Abbey. You will see the ruins of Barden Tower on the right. The gateway is signposted.

Opening times
Open every day except Monday, from the beginning of April (or Easter) to October. Open Bank Holiday Mondays. Tuesdays open in July and August, Wednesday–Sunday, 10.30 am–5.30 pm.

Local Interest:
Bolton Abbey is 3 miles away. Lovely riverside and moorland walks. Strid Wood (Special Site of Scientific Interest SSSI) is a mile away.

The tearooms lie in the heart of the beautiful Yorkshire Dales, in the 15th century Priest's house next to the ruins of Barden Tower. Since establishing the business here in 1991, Robert and Jo have built up a regular trade with summer visitors to the area.

You can take tea either outside overlooking the ruins or inside in the Oak room – so called because of its oak beamed ceiling and magnificent oak dressers which house a fine collection of antique Willow Pattern meat platters (echoed in the crockery used in the tearoom). Many people comment on the wonderfully relaxed atmosphere of the Oak Room with its historic features and gentle period background music.

Light refreshments are served throughout the day. Afternoon Tea is always popular, both in summer when sultana and lemon scones with jam and cream are a particular favourite, and in winter months when customers prefer toasted crumpets or fruit loaf by the log fire.

The water from the shop's moorland spring makes fantastic tea and some customers even bring bottles to fill so that they can take some away to enjoy at home. *Teas served:* Traditional Blend, Assam, Darjeeling, Earl Grey, Lapsang Souchong, Sri Lanka Golden. *Herbal infusions are also available.*

BETTYS CAFE TEA ROOMS

Manager: Nick Carroll

1 Parliament Street, Harrogate
North Yorkshire HG1 2QU
Tel: 01423 502746   Fax: 01423 565191

Directions
Bettys is located on the main route through the centre of Harrogate from Leeds to Ripon, opposite the War Memorial and overlooking Montpelier Gardens.

Opening times
Open all year.
Monday–Sunday, 9 am–9 pm.

Awards
1990, 91, 92 & 93 Tea Council Award of Excellence
1994 Tea Council Top Tea Place of The Year
Egon Ronay recommended

Local Interest:
Wander around Harrogate's wide selection of interesting shops, or walk through Valley Gardens and Harlow Carr Botanical Gardens. Three miles away in Knaresborough, see the oldest chemist's shop in England and visit Mother Shipton's Cave, the home of a 15th century prophet.

The Harrogate branch of Bettys was the first tearoom opened by Frederick Belmont in 1919. The young confectioner arrived from Switzerland and settled in North Yorkshire where he found the clear air very much to his liking. His natural talent for creating exceptionally good cakes and his Swiss flair for hospitality were the perfect combination to build a thriving business and very soon he opened more shops in other Yorkshire towns. Today, the company is still owned by direct descendents of Frederick's family, now half Swiss, half Yorkshire, but still no-one knows the identity of Betty! Frederick Belmont's guiding principle was, "If we want things just right, we have to make them ourselves" and today, Bettys Bakery still makes all the cakes, pastries, chocolates, breads, rolls, fruit loaves, scones and muffins, and all dishes on the menu are freshly prepared on the premises.

Teas and coffees are specially imported and blended by Bettys sister company, Taylors of Harrogate. A café pianist plays every evening from 6 pm to 9 pm. *Teas served:* Tea Room Blend, Special Estate Darjeeling, Special Estate Tippy Assam, Earl Grey, Lapsang Souchong, Yunnan Flowery Orange Pekoe, China Gui Hua, Mountains of the Moon, Zulu, Iced Tea in summer. *Fruit flavoured and herbal teas are also offered.*

Bettys Cafe Tea Rooms

Manager: Hilary Stammers

32–34 The Grove, Ilkley
West Yorkshire LS29 9EE
Tel: 01943 608029   Fax: 01943 816723

Directions
Bettys is in Ilkley town centre, backing on to the main Pay and Display car park and not far from the station and tourist information centre.

Opening times
Open all year.
Monday–Sunday, 9 am–6 pm.

Awards
1990, 91 & 92 Tea Council Award of Excellence
1993 Tea Council Top Tea Place of The Year
Egon Ronay recommended

Local Interest:
Visit the Victorian Arcade, the Manor House Museum, the Kings Hall and Winter Gardens and drive or walk out of town across Ilkley Moor to see some of Yorkshire's most impressive countryside.

This is one of the four hugely successful Bettys Cafe Tea Rooms in Yorkshire and the special feature of this branch is the wonderful, colourful collection of over 200 teapots that are arranged on a high shelf that runs all round the tearoom.

The light and sunny tearoom stands in an attractive tree-lined Victorian boulevard and has some lovely stained glass windows that were specially commissioned in the 1980s when the shop was redeveloped. They depict some of the wild flowers that are found on the Yorkshire Moors and the view through them is to Ilkley Moor in the distance.

This is a haven for ramblers who reach the town tired and in need of refreshment after walking for miles across the rugged, wind-swept moorland. They and other visitors can relax and enjoy the fabulous selection of pastries, breads and cakes that come fresh from Bettys bakery. To add to the attraction, a pianist plays every Friday, Saturday and Sunday from 4.30–6 pm. *Teas served:* Tea Room Blend, Special Estate Darjeeling, Special Estate Tippy Assam, Earl Grey, Lapsang Souchong, Yunnan Flower Orange Pekoe, China Gui Hua, Mountains of the Moon, Zulu, Iced Tea (blend of Earl Grey and Ceylon) in summer. *Fruit flavoured and herbal teas are also offered.*

Bettys Cafe Tea Rooms

Manager: Lindsay Judd

**188 High Street, Northallerton
North Yorkshire DL7 8LF
Tel: 01609 775154
Fax: 01609 777552**

Directions
**Bettys is situated in the town centre, in the
main shopping street.**

Opening times
Open all year. Monday–Saturday,
9 am–5.30 pm. Sunday, 10 am–5.30 pm.

Awards
1987   Tea Council Top Tea Place of The Year
1990   Tea Council Award of Excellence
Egon Ronay recommended

Local Interest:
*The town has a market every Wednesday and some
interesting shops. It is a good centre for walking and is
five miles from Old Motherley, one of the best walks in
the area.*

This is the smallest of the four branches of Bettys and it is a real treasure, tucked away in the Saxon market town of Northallerton. It is said that Roman soldiers once marched along the Great North Road that passes very close by and the town is mentioned in the Doomsday Book so there is lots of history here. It was in this delightful setting that Bettys opened the most recent addition to their chain of fantastic Yorkshire tea shops. The company is still owned by the family of the founder, Frederick Belmont, and teas and coffees are specially blended for the shops by the sister company, Taylors of Harrogate.

The sunny golden room here in Northallerton is small and intimate and decorated with Art Deco mirrors and antique teapots. As you step inside the red brick Georgian building, your attention will be caught by the selection of wonderful cakes and pastries that fill the counter. How does one ever decide what to eat? There are just so many delicious things to try. More than one visit is recommended in order to work your way through at least some of the selection. *Teas served:* Tea Room Blend, Special Estate Darjeeling, Special Estate Tippy Assam, Earl Grey, Lapsang Souchong, Yunnan Flower Orange Pekoe, China Gui Hua, Mountains of the Moon, Zulu. *Fruit flavoured and herbal teas are also offered.*

BETTYS CAFE TEA ROOMS

Manager: Sally Carter

**6–8 St Helen's Square, York
North Yorkshire YO1 2QP
Tel: 01904 659142
Fax: 01904 627050**

Directions
**Bettys is located in the city centre, just round
the corner from York Minster.**

Opening times
Open all year.
Monday–Sunday, 9 am–9 pm.

Award
Egon Ronay recommended

Local Interest:
*From Bettys you can walk to the Minster, The Treasurer's
House, Merchant Taylors' Hall, Yorkshire Museum and
Museum Gardens, St Mary's Abbey, the Railway War
Memorial, Waxworks, open air market and lots more.*

The York branch of Bettys is the most continental in style since its huge picture windows that overlook the cobbled streets allow customers to almost feel part of the pavement scene. The sense of space and light is also due to the fact the tearooms were styled by the designers of the interior of the ocean liner, the Queen Mary. When Frederick Belmont, the originator of Bettys in 1919, took his first holiday from the dedicated hard work of running his first cafe tearoom in Harrogate, he treated himself to a ticket for the maiden voyage of the famous liner and fell in love with the contours and shapes of the lounges and dining rooms, cabins and stairways. On his return he commissioned the same design team for his new cafe in York's town centre and the artists created a light and airy room on the ground floor and a darker, richer effect in the oak-panelled room downstairs.

Today, the cakes and pastries are as irresistible as they were then and customers return again and again. An added attraction is the café pianist who plays every evening from 6 pm to 9 pm. *Teas served:* Tea Room Blend, Special Estate Darjeeling, Special Estate Tippy Assam, Earl Grey, Lapsang Souchong, Yunnan Flowery Orange Pekoe, China Gui Hua, Mountains of the Moon, Zulu. *Fruit flavoured and herbal teas are also offered.*

BULLIVANT OF YORK

Owner: Christine Bullivant

**15 Blake Street
York YO1 2QJ
Tel: 01904 671311**

Directions
From York Minster, walk along Duncombe Place to the cross roads. Turn left into Blake Street and the tea shop is about 150 yards along.

Opening times
Open all year except Sundays.
Monday–Saturday, 9.30 am–5 pm.

Local Interest:
The tea shop is near all of York's main attractions - the Minster, St Mary's Abbey, York Castle, Yorkshire Museum and Museum Gardens.

Christine Bullivant's main concern is that her customers should feel pampered and relaxed in her charming, intimate Victorian-style tearoom. The pretty pink decor, the pink Lloyd Loom chairs and the fascinating variety of antique objects make it a very special place to stop for lunch or tea. A peaceful courtyard provides more seating in good weather and here you can sit surrounded by tubs full of flowers and climbing plants.

Bullivant's menu offers an incredible range of sandwiches, club sandwiches, luncheons of wonderful cheeses, pies, patés and roast meats, and at tea-time all the traditional favourites are on offer – cinnamon toast, delicious scones with Cornish clotted cream, toasted teacakes, hot buttered crumpets and a really special dark fruit cake that is served with Wensleydale cheese.

The shop also houses a section of unusual and very pretty accessories for the home and if you are interested, Christine's helpful staff will bring any of the items to your table so that you can decide in comfort what to buy to take home with you. *Teas served:* Select Blend, Traditional English, Earl Grey, Ceylon, China, Assam, Darjeeling, Lapsang Souchong, Rose Pouchong, Decaffeinated, Lemon. *Fruit flavoured teas and herbal infusions are also available.*

CLARK'S TEAROOMS

Owners: Judy and Gerald Clark

**Market Place, Easingwold
Yorkshire YO6 3AG
Tel: 01347 823143**

Directions
Easingwold is on the A19, 13 miles north of York and ten miles south of Thirsk. Clark's

Tearooms is situated in the market square just off the A19.

Opening times
Open all year except Sundays.
Monday, Tuesday, Wednesday, 10 am–5 pm.
Thursday and Saturday, 9.30 am–5 pm.
Friday, 9 am–5 pm.
Sunday, closed.

Local Interest:
Easingwold is in the Vale of York and close to the North Yorkshire Moors and so is a good centre for walking and cycling.

All the breads, pastries and cakes served and sold at Clark's Tearooms are made at the shop's bakery that was set up about 70 years ago in an early 17th century building by the grandmother of the current owner, Gerald Clark. She started her business by baking scones to sell through the window of her house, as it was then, to cyclists passing through the town on their way to York or the Yorkshire moors. The house was later converted to become a bakery, shop and a small cafe, but the main tearoom is now in the Market Place in the centre of town.

The pretty pink and green shop is divided into three rooms with a smokers' parlour at the back. Local artists display their paintings on the walls and traditional dark furniture is set off by rose-covered curtains and tablecloths. The menu offers sandwiches, home-baked savouries, breads and cakes, and local specialities such as Wensleydale cheese, Yorkshire Fruit Cake, Yorkshire Curd Tarts and delicious fruit pies with cream. If you would like to buy some of them to take home, Judy and Gerald Clark have a shop on the opposite side of the street which sells all their breads, pastries and cakes. *Teas served:* House Blend, Earl Grey, Darjeeling. *Fruit flavoured teas are also offered.*

DE VERE OULTON HALL HOTEL

Owner: De Vere Hotels
Manager: Michael Thaw

Rothwell Lane
Oulton, Leeds
Yorkshire LS26 8HN
Tel: 01532 821000
Fax: 01532 828066

Directions
Take junction 42 or 43 off the M1 or junction 30 off the M62. Follow signs for Oulton.

Opening times
Open all year.
Tea is served in the Drawing Room which is open Monday–Sunday, 10 am–6 pm.

Local Interest:
The hotel's Leisure Club offers a swimming pool, a golf course, a gym, squash courts, sauna and steam room. Also visit York, the Yorkshire Dales and the National Photographic Museum in Bradford.

Oulton Hall stands on the high ground above the Yorkshire village of Rothwell. It was originally a simple farmhouse but was rebuilt as an elegant hall in the early 19th century. After a major fire in 1850, the house was again remodelled and extended, making it truly a mansion, complete with Great Hall and Gallery. During this century, it gradually fell into disrepair and was threatened with demolition until first Leeds City Council bought it and then De Vere Hotels rescued it. The wonderfully restored Hall stands in the most beautiful parkland, and around the house are 19th century gardens that are Grade II listed in the English Register of Historic Gardens.

This elegant setting creates a sense of stepping back in time to the days when afternoon tea was the highlight of many people's day. Tea at Oulton Hall, an AA 5 star hotel, is served in the Drawing Room where the menu offers a selection of mouthwatering sandwiches (grilled prawns with Marie Rose sauce, turkey breast with cranberry sauce and crisp lettuce), delicious cakes, including a fruit cake that is served with Wensleydale cheese, and scones with clotted cream and strawberry jam. The very friendly, welcoming atmosphere will ensure that you really feel at home. *Teas served:* House Blend, Ceylon, Darjeeling, Assam, Earl Grey, Lapsang Souchong. *Camomile infusion is also offered.*

MAD HATTER TEA SHOP

Owners: Margaret and Brian Boshier

Market Place, Masham
Near Ripon, North Yorkshire
HG4 4EA
Tel: 01765 689129

Directions
Masham is 20 miles north of Harrogate on the A61 between Glasshouses and Jervaulx and 8 miles west of the A1 of the B6267. The tea shop is in the heart of the town in the market square.

Opening times
Open all year except Thursday. Monday, Tuesday, Wednesday, Friday, Saturday, 10 am–5 pm. Sunday, 11 am–5 pm. Thursday, closed.

Local Interest:
Masham has a unique September sheep fair every year. There are also two breweries with visitor centres and guided tours, a glass works and pottery, all very close to the town centre. The town is at the entrance to the Yorkshire Dales and so is an ideal location for walking and trips out into the wonderful countryside.

Margaret and Brian Boshier thought they were taking semi-retirement when they opened their tea shop in the heart of Masham, but with a two-bedroomed Bed & Breakfast business and the busy tearooms, they are probably busier than ever. When they took over the tall, three-storey building which faces Masham's old-fashioned market square, it was still a house and they have converted the lower floor to create the friendly and welcoming tea shop. Brian's past days of playing cricket and a passion for collecting cricket memorabilia has led to an interesting array of cricket bats, cricket photos, cigarette cards and other cricketing bits and pieces in one of the two tearooms.

Margaret's menu is full of delicious home-made savouries – Welsh rarebit, open sandwiches, and tasty hot pots – and really unusual cakes such as parsnip and pecan, pineapple and ginger, coconut and lime. Her range of home-baked scones includes fruit, date and walnut, cheese, and wholemeal. So, before heading off to find out about beer making at one of the local breweries, indulge in the best beverage of all with one of her special treats. *Teas served:* Yorkshire Tea, Earl Grey, Darjeeling, Ceylon, Assam, Kenya. *Fruit flavoured and herbal teas are also available.*

TAYLORS IN STONEGATE

Manager: Janet Todd

**46 Stonegate, York
North Yorkshire YO1 2AS
Tel: 01904 622865
Fax: 01904 640348**

Directions
Taylors is very close to York Minster in Stonegate which is off Petergate.

Opening times
Open all year.
Monday–Sunday, 9 am–5.30 pm.

Awards
1991, 92 & 93   Tea Council Award of Excellence
Egon Ronay recommended

Local Interest:
Within walking distance of the tearoom are York Minster, The Treasurer's House, the Merchant Taylors' Hall, St Mary's Abbey, Yorkshire Museum and Museum Gardens, Waxworks, York Castle and Museum, Cliffords Tower, Coppergate Shopping Centre and so much more.

It is evident from the 18th century name of a nearby snickleway, 'Coffee Yard', that Stonegate has had associations with coffee since long before Taylors set up in business as tea and coffee merchants in 1886. Two brothers, Charles and Llewellyn Taylor, established the family firm in what is now a Grade II listed building in the heart of medieval York. Over the years, the brothers acquired a discerning clientele and even supplied the coffee for King Edward VII's coronation. Today, it is the very epitome of a perfect English tearoom.

In 1962, Taylors became part of the Bettys family business and is one of five world-famous tearooms with an outstanding selection of teas and coffees, chocolates, breads, cakes and Yorkshire specialities such as Fat Rascals, Spiced Yorkshire Teacakes and Yorkshire Curd Tart.

Once you have tried and become addicted to the excellent foods and teas, you can have a regular supply sent by post by telephoning Harrogate 01423 886055. *Teas served:* Stonegate Tearoom Blend, Choice Assam, Special Estate Tippy Assam, Fine Darjeeling BOP, Vintage Darjeeling, Fine Ceylon BOP, Ceylon Orange Pekoe, Earl Grey, Keemun, Lapsang Souchong, Mountains of the Moon, China Gui Hua, Japanese Cherry, Zulu. *Flavoured and herbal teas are also offered.*

N O R T H   W E S T
R E G I O N A L   M A P

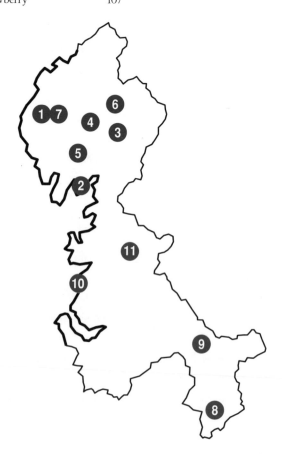

ABRAHAM'S TEA ROOM

Manager: Rosalind Bunting

**George Fisher Ltd
2 Borrowdale Road
Keswick, Cumbria CA12 5DA
Tel: 017687 72178**

Directions
Abraham's is on the 2nd floor of George Fisher
Ltd on the corner of Lake Road and
Borrowdale Road in Keswick.

Opening times
Open all year except Christmas Day,
Boxing Day and Easter Sunday.
Monday–Friday, 10 am–5.30 pm.
Saturday, 9.30 am–5.30 pm.
Sunday, 10.30 am–4.30 pm.

Local Interest:
*Keswick, situated at the north end of Lake
Derwentwater, is one of the main centres in the Lake
District for walking and climbing.*

Both Abraham's and the shop in which it is housed, George Fisher Ltd, are true Keswick establishments. The Abraham brothers, George and Ashley, were avid late 19th century mountain climbers who also took photographs of other climbers. Their father ran his photography business in this building from 1887. In 1967, George Fisher took over the premises from Geoffrey Abraham to extend his business selling and hiring climbing equipment.

So the tea room has a direct link with the wonderful hills and mountains it is surrounded by and which can be seen from the windows. The floor is of riven local slate, giving the feel of a real mountain climbing hut, and on the walls are original Abraham photographs.

The menu provides everything climbers and walkers could possibly want – hot drinks (some in generous mugs), gluhwein to 'bring back Alpine memories', beers, wines, teas and, of course, good wholesome robust local dishes for all times of the day. At tea-time, there are scones, crumpets, muffins, pies, cakes and ice creams. Because Abraham's specialises in healthy eating, several of the recipes use low fat and sugar content. *Teas served:* Assam, Darjeeling, English Breakfast, Earl Grey, Indian, Decaffeinated, House Blend. *Herbal infusions also available.*

HAZELMERE CAFE & BAKERY

Owners: Dorothy & Ian Studley

1 Yewbarrow Terrace
Grange-over-Sands
Cumbria LA11 6ED
Tel: 015395 32972
Fax: 015395 32972

Directions
When coming into Grange-over-Sands on the B5277, you will pass Grange station on the left. Shortly after this, there is a mini-roundabout. Take the first exit and the Café is about 25 yards along, on the right.

Opening times
Open all year.
10 am–4.30 pm in winter,
9.30 am–5.30 pm in summer.

Local Interest:
The Hazelmere overlooks Grange's famous ornamental gardens. The bay is a perfect place for walks on the sand and a short ride by car will take you up into the Lake District.

Grange-over-Sands is one of those towns that just would not be complete without a high-class tea shop, and the Hazelmere, set in a parade of Victorian shops fronted by a beautiful ornate glass and cast iron verandah provides the perfect venue for tea, and also manages to recapture the spirit of traditional tea-time. Dorothy and Ian Studley specialise in home-made quality food using only the best ingredients, including free-range eggs and fresh cream. They make everything on the premises and like to include a mixture of local specialities as well as their own original recipes.

Since the Studleys also have their own bakery and bakery shop and were winners of Bake '93 for the North West region, you can be absolutely sure that you will not be disappointed by the selection of real treats – Cumberland rum nicky, Yorkshire curd tart, Westmoreland pepper cake, and sandwiches filled with smoked Cumberland cheese with pear and kiwi fruit, turkey breast with home-made carrot, cheese and onion salad, and cheddar cheese with home-made apricot chutney. *Teas served:* House Lakeland Blend, Darjeeling, Earl Grey, Assam, featuring different speciality teas (e.g. Boh Tea Plantations, Cameron Highlands) which change from time to time. *Herbal infusions are also available.*

NEW VILLAGE TEA ROOMS

Owner: Christine Evans

**Orton, Penrith
Cumbria CA10 3RH
Tel: 015396 24886**

Directions
Leave the M6 at junction 38 and take the Appleby road. In Orton, take the Shap road in front of the George Hotel. The Tea Rooms are straight ahead, opposite the stores and Post Office, where the road turns left and leaves the village.

Opening times
Open all year.
July–August, 10 am–6 pm. April, May, June, September, October, 10 am–5 pm.
November, March, 10.30 am–4.30 pm. 🚭

Local Interest:
Orton is an interesting village with buildings dating back to the 17th and 18th centuries. It is an ideal centre for visits to the Lake District, the Yorkshire Dales, the North Pennines, the Border Country and Morecambe Bay. The Wainwright 'Coast to Coast' walk (from St Bees to Robin Hood's Bay) touches the village.

The New Village Tea Rooms are housed in an 18th century building which has had a varied history and was most recently a cottage. The downstairs tearoom was once the cottage living room and the kitchen is open to the friendly area where customers now sit to enjoy their tea. This means that they can chat to the staff while their food is being prepared and feel really at home.

On hot summer days, the tearooms remain cool and comfortable but sunlovers can bask outside in the pretty cottage garden. In winter, an open coal fire keeps visitors warm and cosy and creates a haven for walkers. Californian 'Coast to Coast' walkers who visited when walking west to east in 1992 and again when walking east to west in 1994, said that the sticky toffee pudding was the best in the country and took the recipe home, vowing to keep it a secret for ever.

All the food is prepared on the premises using traditional methods and locally produced quality ingredients. The menu offers a wide range of home-made cakes, tempting desserts, sandwiches and hot lunch dishes in a totally smoke-free environment. *Teas served:* Earl Grey, Ceylon, Darjeeling, Assam, Lapsang Souchong, PG Tips. *Fruit flavoured teas and herbal infusions are also offered.*

SHARROW BAY COUNTRY HOUSE HOTEL

Owners: Francis Coulson & Brian Sack

**Lake Ullswater, Howtown
Cumbria CA10 2LZ
Tel: 017684 86301   Fax: 017684 86349**

Directions
Leave the M6 at Junction 40 and travel west on the A66 to Keswick and Ullswater. At the roundabout, take the 1st exit on to the A592 to Ullswater. At the T-junction, turn left into Pooley Bridge. Travel through the village and take the right fork at the church, signposted to Howtown. At the crossroads, turn right to Howtown and follow Lake Road for 2 miles.

Opening times
Open from the end of February to the end of November. Monday–Sunday, 7.30 am–10.30 pm.

Local Interest:
Sharrow Bay Hotel is positioned right on the edge of Lake Ullswater and there are spectacular walks in all directions. Two old steamers carry passengers up and down the lake and stop at Pooley Bridge and Howtown, both quite close to the hotel.

When Francis Coulson opened Sharrow Bay Country House Hotel in 1949, food was rationed, petrol was rationed, there was no motorway, and the Lake District wasn't considered to be very fashionable. But, Francis very quickly gained a reputation for wonderful afternoon teas with cakes and scones that he made to recipes taught him by his mother. Today, the reputation has grown, not just for afternoon tea but for the wonderful accommodation, gracious and caring staff, a calm and peaceful ambience, the huge traditional English breakfasts and amazing dinners.

Afternoon Tea remains the real speciality of the house. Just as in the early days, everything is baked on the premises and the superb cakes include Grasmere gingerbread, genoese cream sponges, dainty tartlets, lemon cake that is absolutely soaked with sugary juice, and meringues.

Tea is served in two lounges and the conservatory, with Minton china on elegant silver trays. If you choose the drawing room, the view across Lake Ullswater is probably one of the finest in England. Because the hotel is so popular for tea, do book ahead if you can. *Teas served:* English Breakfast, Darjeeling, Ceylon, Indian, Earl Grey, Lapsang Souchong, China. *A variety of infusions are also available.*

SHEILA'S COTTAGE

Owners: Janice and Stewart Greaves

The Slack, Ambleside
Cumbria LA22 9DQ
Tel: 015394 33079
Fax: 015394 34488

Directions
**Turn under an archway off the Market Place
and walk down a narrow lane to the tea shop.**

Opening times
Open February–end December. Closed January.
Monday, 11 am–5 pm. Tuesday–Saturday,
11 am–9.30 pm. Sunday (February, March,
April and November, December), 11 am–5 pm.

Awards
1990   Tea Council Award of Excellence
Egon Ronay recommended

Local Interest:
*Ambleside is a typical lakeland town at the head
of Lake Windermere, the largest of the lakes. Visit Bridge
House, thought to be the 17th century summer house of a
mansion that has long since disappeared, and Adrian
Sankey's glass blowing workshop. Steamers leave from
Waterhead for Lakeside and Bowness.*

In the 1950s, Stewart and Janice Greaves owned a holiday cottage in the Ambleside area which was called Sheila's Cottage, after Stewart's mother, and in which they spent many happy times. So when they bought an empty cottage in the town in the 60s they used the same name and have been in business there for 30 very successful years. The cottage is a typical 250-year-old lakeland, slate-roofed building which was used in Victorian days as shelter for coachmen whose passengers stayed in the smarter inns in the main square and whose horses were stabled just down The Slack where the blacksmith once had his workshop. Today, the interior of the quaint cottage and the adjoining barn is typical lakeland cottage style, with papered walls and dark country furniture.

The Greaves have also kept a traditional feel to their menu and make their own breads and muffins with local flour that is ground at the nearby Eskdale Mill. Their Borrowdale tea bread is made with fruit steeped in tea and is served with a local tangy crumbly Lancashire cheese. A dessert not to be missed is Witherslack Damson Cobbler made with local fruit and served hot with whipped cream. *Teas served:* Ceylon, Darjeeling, Broken Orange Pekoe, Earl Grey, Keemun.

THE VILLAGE BAKERY

Owner: Andrew Whitley

Melmerby, Penrith
Cumbria CA10 1HE
Tel: 01768 881515   Fax: 01768 881848

Directions
Melmerby is ten miles from Junction 40 on the M6. Take the A66 eastbound to the next roundabout, then take the A686 to Alston. Continue along the A686 for ten miles. The

Village Bakery is on the left hand side as you go through the village.

Opening times
Open all year. Monday–Saturday, 8.30 am–5 pm. Sunday and Bank Holidays, 9.30 am–5 pm. In January and February, please check before visiting. 🚭

Awards
1987, 1992   Egon Ronay recommended

Local Interest:
The Craft Gallery at the Bakery sells bread crocks, bread knives, prints and postcards of local subjects, hand-knitted jumpers and handmade tableware. The village is at the edge of the north Pennine Hills with its fells, moors and forests.

The Village Bakery was established in 1976 when Lis and Andrew Whitley converted the 200-year-old stone barn next to their house in Melmerby into a bakery, restaurant and craft gallery. In 1977, they built a wood-fired brick oven whose gentle release of heat produces wonderfully satisfying flavours and textures in the breads, rolls, pies and cakes.

Their products were so good and proved so popular that in 1991 a new bakehouse was built with a larger and more efficient brick oven and a surrounding greenhouse to capture the waste heat and create a propagation area for plants. These are then raised in the five acre organic smallholding at the back

of the bakery which supplies the restaurant with fresh vegetables and fruit.

The flour and other ingredients are grown in accordance with Soil Association agricultural standards and some of the wheat is stoneground at the local watermill. The list of specialities is impressive and appeals to a wide public including supermarkets and smaller shops who order regularly. Try Borrowdale tea bread, Grasmere gingerbread, rich fruit cake, wholemeal scones, gluten-free chocolate almond cake and many more in the friendly atmosphere of the old barn. *Teas served:* Ceylon, China, Darjeeling, Earl Grey, Organic Indian Ocean. *Fruit flavoured teas are also offered.*

THE WILD STRAWBERRY

Owners: James & Margaret Wilkinson

**54 Main Street
Keswick
Cumbria CA12 5JS
Tel: 017687 74399**

Directions
The tea shop is situated on Keswick's Main
Street, near the Post Office, just off the lower
end of the market square, with good views of
the Moot Hall.

Opening times
Open all year except 2 weeks in February.
Monday, Tuesday, Thursday, Friday, Saturday,
10 am–5 pm. Wednesday, 10 am–5 pm in season.
Sunday, 12 noon–5 pm.

Local Interest:
*Keswick is the largest town in the Lake District National Park
and is an ideal centre for enjoying the area. Also visit the
Cumberland Pencil Museum, the Motor Museum and the 18th
century Moot Hall. There is a traders' market every Saturday
in the Market Square and every December, a Victorian Fair.*

The friendly cheery tearoom is housed in a 17th century cottage that was once a Cumberland pencil-maker's workshop, and still has its oak beams and flagged floor made from local green slate. The floor of the upstairs room is covered with a carpet made from the wool of Herdwick sheep made famous by Beatrix Potter, and the strawberry theme of the cottage name is continued in the designs for the curtains and the bone china tableware which is specially made for the tearoom. The interior of the cottage is enhanced by photos and personally embroidered pictures, giving a lovely homely feel.

James and Margaret Wilkinson have 35 years of experience in the catering trade and both play an active part in the tearoom, which is very popular with locals and tourists alike. Freshly-baked home-made fayre – and especially the delicious scones and sticky toffee pudding – make choosing a really difficult pleasure! The tearoom's speciality is a fatless and sugar-free fruit tea bread. *Teas served:* House Blend, Assam, Darjeeling, Earl Grey. *Various herbal teas are also available.*

BROOK FARM TEA ROOMS

Owners: Sue and Dave Goodwin

Brook Farm, Repton
Derbyshire DE65 6FW
Tel: 01283 702215

Directions
From the A38, take the turning to Willington. In Willington, follow signs to Repton. Turn left at the monument island and the tearoom is 150 yards away on the left and well sign-posted from the road.

Opening times
Open all year except for 1 week including 25th December and up to New Year. Monday–Sunday, 10.15 am–5 pm.

Award
Egon Ronay recommended

Local Interest:
The main part of Repton village was designated a conservation area in 1969 and there are 40 listed buildings. Visit the Crypt, the final resting place of the Mercian kings who lived here from the 7th–9th centuries, and Repton School, established in 1557. Surrounding countryside is excellent for walking, riding and cycling.

The old sandstone and brick barn that houses Brook Farm Tea Rooms has, over the years, served many functions as part of the working farm. Now, its A-framed wooden roof, white walls, wood-panelled walls and Rayburn stove create a cosy, farmhouse atmosphere where friendly, thoughtful waitresses serve you with a ready smile. The large patio windows allow visitors a view of a grassy bank that slopes gently down to the brook and of the courtyard where calves and other small farm animals are kept in winter.

Sue and Dave Goodwin are very concerned that their customers feel relaxed and comfortable while here and their garden, well away from main roads and with plenty of seating on the lawns, is a quiet and safe place for families. And, because everything is on the flat and easily accessible, it is a perfect place for visitors who find stairs difficult or are wheelchair-bound.

The food is quality, home-baking that appeals to everyone, and children (and quite possibly adults too) will love the farmhouse dairy ice creams that tempt you with such flavours as lemon meringue, melon and ginger, black-berry and rum and raisin. *Teas served:* Traditional Typhoo, Earl Grey, Darjeeling, English Breakfast, Assam, Yorkshire. *Fruit flavoured and herbal teas are also offered.*

THE COTTAGE TEA ROOM

Owners: Bill and Betty Watkins

**3 Fennel Street, Ashford-in-the-Water
Near Bakewell, Derbyshire DE45 1QF
Tel: 01629 812488**

Directions
Ashford-in-the-Water lies on the A6, two miles
north of Bakewell and eight miles south of
Buxton Spa. The tearoom is just above the ford
by the ancient sheepwash bridge.

Opening times
Open all year except Tuesdays and F, one week in mid-September, Christma╮ ╮y, Boxing Day and New Years Day. Monday, Wednesday, Thursday, 2.30–5 pm. Tuesday and Friday, closed. Saturday and Sunday, 10.30 am–12 noon, 2.30–5 pm.

Award
Egon Ronay recommended

Local Interest:
Ashford-in-the-Water, once part of the Duke of Devonshire's Chatsworth Estate, is considered to be the jewel of The Peak District National park. Five bridges span the River Wye (famous amongst anglers). The Norman church contains examples of the local coloured marble and there is a carefully restored 14th century tithe barn.

This exquisite cottage stands beside an old Roman road, Fennel Street, the old drovers' road from Inverness to London. Like the unspoilt conservation village, with its buildings in mellow Derbyshire stone, the special feature of Bill and Betty Watkins' Cottage Tea Room is its unchanging quality. In summertime, old-fashioned roses clamber up the cottage walls and the outbuildings are ablaze with troughs of flowers raised by the green-fingered proprietors. Every season has its appeal – from daffodil spring to golden autumn – but it is in wintertime that the windows glow invitingly while the open fire ensures a warm welcome to visitors.

The accent is on genuine home cooking. There is a wonderful array of traditional English cakes and hand-kneaded breads, and a variety of feather-light scones is baked daily. The warm cheesy herb scones are a great favourite on winter days. Six set meals are served and you can choose anything from a simple pot of tea and a slice of cake to the full afternoon tea.

Teas served: In addition to the specially blended House tea, an extensive selection of leaf teas is available, including 6 China, 5 Ceylon, 3 Indian, Kenyan, Formosa Oolong, Russian Caravan, Earl Grey and English Breakfast. *A range of herbal infusions is also provided.*

NOSTALGIA TEAROOMS

Owner: Ann Couzens

215–217 Lord Street, Southport
Lancashire PR8 1NZ
Tel: 01704 501294

Directions
Nostalgia is opposite the Tourist Information Centre, on the first floor of the black and white building, above The Early Learning Centre.

Opening times
Open all year. Monday, open only in July and August, 9.30 am–5 pm. Tuesday–Saturday, 9.30 am–5 pm. Sunday, 10 am–5 pm.

Local Interest:
Southport has a steam locomotive museum, the Atkinson Art Gallery, Warfarers Arcade with its statue of Red Rum and Marine Lake with fun fair, boating, walks and a miniature railway.

Ann Couzens had already enjoyed considerable success with her first tearoom in Birkdale before opening this Southport branch in one of the town's typical Victorian arcades. Ann used to be a catering teacher in one of the local schools and several of her staff are past pupils who she has trained individually in the traditional preparation, presentation and service of food and in customer relations. She also designed the furniture and the interior decoration herself so that the large airy room would look absolutely right. Styled on a conservatory, with bamboo chairs and a colour scheme in pale pink and green, this is an elegant and restful place to take tea, where waitresses in pretty Victorian black and white costumes look after you in the old-fashioned way.

The generous menu which is supplemented by a daily blackboard, includes modern as well as traditional cakes and the Pavlova and choux gâteau are extremely tempting. And there are ice cream sundaes with exotic names such as Mississippi Steamboat and Singapore Surprise. But, even if you settle for just a cup of tea and a flapjack, you are bound to enjoy the reassuring Englishness of the experience. *Teas served:* Yorkshire Gold Premium, English Breakfast, Earl Grey, Darjeeling, Ceylon, Assam. *Fruit flavoured and herbal teas are also offered.*

THE TOBY JUG TEA SHOP

Owners: Peter and Marie Ireland

**20 King Street, Whalley
Clitheroe, Lancashire
BB7 9SL
Tel: 01254 823298
Fax: 01254 823298**

Directions

The Toby Jug is in the main street of Whalley Village, by the bridge over the River Calder.

Opening times

Open all year except Mondays and Tuesdays.
Monday and Tuesday, closed.
Wednesday, Thursday and Friday, 10 am–4.30 pm.
Saturday and Sunday, 10.30 am–5 pm. 🚭

Local Interest:

Whalley is an attractive village with some good shops and a parish church that has some interesting Saxon crosses in the churchyard. The Cistercian Abbey is mostly in ruins but the Chapter House is still used as a retreat.

Three hundred years ago, the house that is today the Toby Jug Tea Shop was King Street Farm and stood on Whalley Village's important main road along which stagecoaches rumbled on their way to the Fylde coast. It was here that pilgrims to the mother church of the largest parish in Lancashire crossed the River Calder and, no doubt, found it a good resting place, for the babbling waters that run through the picturesque village were said in 1547 to be "rich in salmons, troutes and other fine fishes".

Inside the tearoom, the oak beams, wonderful old stone fireplaces and wooden panelling on the upstairs walls hark back to those historic days, creating a very special atmosphere and an idyllic resting place for thirsty travellers in need of a cup of tea.

The menu is packed with delicious lunchtime savouries and sandwich ideas and, for tea, there are scones and an extensive range of tempting cakes, pastries, fruit pies and gateaux – all made on the premises and reminiscent of the baking days of past generations. *Teas served:* Yorkshire Blend, English Breakfast, Ceylon, Darjeeling, Lapsang Souchong, Keemun, Jasmine Blossom, Decaffeinated. *Fruit flavoured and herbal teas are also offered.*

WALES
REGIONAL MAP

BODIDRIS HALL

Manager: Tudor Williams

Llandegla
Wrexham, Clwyd
L11 3AL
Tel: 01978 790434
Fax: 01978 790335

Directions
Llandegla lies at the point where the A525, the A5104 and the A542 meet, about 8 miles due west of Wrexham. Take the A5104 north towards Chester for about 1 mile and Bodidris is on the left, signposted at the top of the drive.

Opening times
Open 24 hours, all year.
Tea is served every day from 2.30–5 pm.
There is also a simpler tea service at all times of the day. (ꜱ)

Local Interest:
The Roman city of Chester, walking trails, cycling, archery, clay pigeon shooting, fishing, falconry, vineyards, heritage trails, tuition days in medieval skills such as tapestry, dance, armour making and heraldry.

This is no ordinary hotel and restaurant. The stone walls of Bodidris Hall have, for nine hundred years, been the site of bloody battles and royal visits, and in Tudor times, became the hunting lodge of Lord Robert Dudley, Earl of Leicester. The hotel is hidden away amongst some of the most beautiful Welsh countryside and is surrounded by landscaped lawns, meadowland and ponds filled with trout. The style of the interior of the house is totally in keeping with its historic past, and there are four-poster beds, open fireplaces with inglenooks and roaring log fires, beamed ceilings and a duelling staircase that dates back to the 16th century.

Afternoon Tea is just one of many culinary treats that the hotel offers. The menu is filled with wonderful savoury dishes and puddings and at tea-time, there are Welsh cakes, traditional Bara Brith fruited loaf, teacakes, scones and shortbread. All the pastries, cakes and preserves are made on the premises and sold under the brand name Celtic Country Foods. To learn about the history of the house, take a guided tour, which lasts an hour, and is followed by a full Cream Tea. *Teas served:* Breakfast, Darjeeling, Earl Grey, Lapsang Souchong, Royalty. *Fruit teas and herbal infusions are also available.*

ST TUDNO HOTEL

Owners: Martin & Janette Bland

**Promenade, Llandudno
Gwynedd LL30 2LP
Tel: 01492 874411
Fax: 01492 860407**

Directions
**From the A55 take the A470 Llandudno
Link road. On reaching the Promenade,
drive towards the Great Orme headland. The**
hotel is directly opposite the pier entrance and
ornamental gardens.

Opening times
Open all year, 7 am–11 pm.

Award
Egon Ronay recommended

Local Interest:
*The town, with its Victorian pier, gardens and beach, is
ideally located for exploring North Wales. Nearby there
are castles, National Trust properties and the world
famous gardens at Bodnant.*

The St Tudno Hotel enjoys a reputation as one of the most luxurious seaside resort hotels in Great Britain and has won an amazing number of awards over the years. Martin and Janette Bland, with their unique flair for hotel keeping and incredibly high standards, really deserve all the accolades. The hotel interiors are wonderfully glamourous, the staff are extremely attentive and the atmosphere is one of charm and warmth and meticulous care. And an extra item of interest is the fact that Alice Liddell, immortalised by Lewis Carroll as the heroine of Alice in Wonderland, stayed at the St Tudno at the age of eight on her first visit to Llandudno in 1861.

In good weather, take tea on the patio and enjoy outstanding views over the bay. In winter, choose one of three beautifully designed lounges. The menu offers two set teas – the Full Afternoon Tea with sandwiches, scones, Bara Brith, Welsh Cakes and home-made cakes; and the De-Luxe Afternoon Tea includes the full afternoon tea and adds smoked salmon sandwiches, strawberries and cream and a glass of champagne. *Teas served:* Assam, Darjeeling, Ceylon, Lapsang Souchong, Decaffeinated, Earl Grey, 2 House Blends – Yorkshire Gold Medal and English Breakfast. *Fruit teas and herbal infusions are also offered.*

GWALIA TEA ROOMS

Owner: Mike Morton

**The Museum of Welsh Life
St Fagans, Cardiff
CF5 6XB
Tel: 01222 566985
Fax: 01222 566985**

Directions
Take exit 33 off the M4 and follow signs to

The Museum of Welsh Life. The tea rooms are within the grounds of the museum.

Opening times
Open all year except Christmas Day, Boxing Day and New Year's Day, 10 am–4.45 pm.

Local Interest:
The tea shop is within the grounds of the Museum of Welsh Life which has a complete Welsh village with blacksmith, school, old cottages, an old photographer's shop and lots more.

Gwalia Tea Rooms are situated on the first floor of Gwalia Stores, a high class department store that was moved stone by stone from the coal-mining village of Ogmore Vale and meticulously rebuilt within the grounds of the Museum of Welsh Life. The interior, once the corn store, is decorated and furnished in the authentic style of the 1920s, with bentwood chairs, old mirrors, a cut glass screen at one end of the room and old photos of the building in its original setting. To get to the tea room, you have to pass through the old-fashioned ironmongery downstairs where you can still buy an old tin bath, if you want to. However, you might be more interested in the jams and pickles and other home-made goodies.

The tea-time menu is as traditional as the shop surroundings and includes, of course, Welsh cakes and Bara Brith, which Mike Morton sends out on mail order to people who tried it once and now want more. And custard slices are a regular treat, again following a tradition from the days when Mr Llewellyn, who ran Gwalia Stores back in Ogmore Vale, baked them every Friday. *Teas served:* Darjeeling, Assam, Ceylon, Earl Grey, Lapsang Souchong, Jasmine, Gunpowder, Oolong, Yunnan, Rose Pouchong. *Fruit flavoured teas and herbal infusions are also available.*

CELTIC FARE TEAROOMS

Owner: Christopher Phillips

**Vernon House, St Julians Street
Tenby, Pembrokeshire SA70 7AS
Tel: 01834 845258**

Directions
Take the A478 into Tenby and the Celtic Tearooms is half way down St Julians Street on the left hand side, very close to the Harbour and Castle Beach.

Opening times
Open all year.
Monday–Sunday, 9.30–5.30 pm.

Award
1993   Tea Council Award of Excellence

Local Interest:
You can walk around the old town walls and visit the 14th century Tudor Merchant's House (now run by The National Trust), the Museum, Lifeboat Station and Aquarium. Fishing trips go from the harbour and boat trips leave every half hour to Caldey Island which is 20 minutes away and has a Cistercian Monastery.

Celtic Fare is a real traditional Welsh tearoom serving home-baked cakes, pastries and savouries of a very high standard. In its first year it won a Tea Council Award of Excellence and deserves to be packed all the time with appreciative, hungry customers.

The attraction starts right at the front door to this eye-catching building where bright hanging baskets surround the pretty door and windows. Inside, there is a feeling of warmth and welcome. The old beams are hung with jugs and teapots, original gas lamps cast a warm glow over the cosy, friendly room and there is a real fire in the Victorian hearth and fresh flowers around the room. The Celtic spirit is heightened by the soothing traditional music playing in the background and the really tempting freshly baked Welsh cakes, hot from the griddle and scones served with lashings of Caldey Island clotted cream and fruity jam.

Light snacks are available all day and you can lunch on Welsh rarebits or Heggarty Pie with crisp bacon topping, or take tea with tangy lemon torte, apple cake and fresh fruit pavlovas. The display on the counter will make it really difficult for you to choose. *Teas served:* House Blend, Earl Grey, Darjeeling, Ceylon, Lapsang Souchong. *Fruit flavoured and herbal teas are also offered.*

THE OLD STATION COFFEE SHOP

Owner: Eileen Minter

Dinas Mawddwy
Machynlleth
Powys SY20 9LS
Tel: 01650 531338

Directions
The A470 (the main North to South Wales road) passes the gate to Meirion Mill by Minllyn Bridge one mile north of the A470 junction with A458 at Mallwyd. The Old Station Coffee Shop is on the right, inside the gate to the Mill.

Opening times
Open March–mid-November.
Monday–Sunday, 9.30 am–5 pm.

Award
Egon Ronay recommended

Local Interest:
Meirion Mill is in what were the old slate engine sheds. The working looms produce cloth and garments that are for sale in the Mill shop. There are walks and climbs in all directions.

The Old Station stands beneath high conifers at the side of a disused railway line in an area of Wales steeped in legend and history and where King Arthur is said to have fought his last battle. Visitors can walk for miles to explore the surrounding Dinas Mawddwy mountains and countryside that create the backdrop for the old station building.

The original waiting room is now two tearooms that still have the old-fashioned station fireplace and are furnished with pine chairs and tables and two Welsh dressers. Outside, on the old platform there are slate tables and teak benches, and the bright colours of fresh flowers, plants in tubs and cascading hanging baskets add their own charm to this lovely setting, while old station signs remind you of the days when steam engines pulled their heavy load of freight or passenger carriages through the breathtaking Welsh scenery.

Of course, Eileen Minter's menu is also deliciously Welsh and the Bara Brith and cheese scones are so good that apparently people come hundreds of miles to taste them. Welsh cakes are on sale in packets so that you can take away a taste of Wales to enjoy at home. *Teas served:* Indian, Darjeeling, Assam, English Breakfast, Earl Grey, China, Decaffeinated. *Herbal tea is also offered.*

SCOTLAND
REGIONAL MAP

ABBEY COTTAGE TEA ROOMS

Owners: Morag McKie and
Jacqui Wilson

**26 Main Street, New Abbey
Dumfries DG2 8BY
Tel: 01387 850377**

Directions
**Take the A710 from Dumfries to New Abbey
(the Solway Coast Road). Abbey Cottage is
beside Sweetheart Abbey. The Village Car Park
is behind.**

Opening times
**Open 1st April–31st October and
weekends to Christmas.
Monday–Sunday, 10 am–5.30 pm.**

Award
Egon Ronay recommended

Local Interest:
*Wander around the Abbey ruins and learn the story of
Lady Devorgilla. Also visit the Shambellie House Museum of
Costume and an 18th century water mill that still operates.*

If you take the Solway Coast Road from Dumfries, you will drive through some wonderful countryside before you find yourself in the quiet village of New Abbey. Here stand the rose-coloured remains of Sweetheart Abbey, built by Lady Devorgilla in the 13th century in memory of her husband, John Balliol, with whom she founded Balliol College, Oxford.

Just across the road from the medieval ruins, 19th century Abbey Cottage offers a warm welcome and a delicious selection of healthy home-made specialities that are served in a friendly, caring, non-smoking environment. Morag McKie and her daughter Jacqui use high-quality local produce and include low-fat and vegetarian options on their menu. Home-made soups, granary breads, Scottish country pâté and tasty sandwiches or salads are perfect for a light lunch, while the tea-time selection includes Jacqui's excellent carrot or banana cake, and plain, wholemeal or fruit scones that are served with Morag's home-made jams. In good weather, enjoy your tea in the garden at the back of the pretty cottage and before leaving, visit the craft shop next door to browse amongst the very attractive range of local pottery, candles and table wares. *Teas served:* Traditional Blend, Assam, Darjeeling, Earl Grey and Decaffeinated. *Fruit flavoured and herbal teas are also offered.*

KIND KYTTOCK'S KITCHEN

Owners: Liz and Bert Dalrymple

**Cross Wynd, Falkland
Fife, KY7 7BE
Tel: 01337 857477**

Directions
Follow signs from the M90 for Falkland Palace. Cross Wynd joins the High Street at the fountain and Mercat Cross.

Opening times
Open all year except Mondays and two weeks from Christmas Day–January 5th.
Tuesday–Sunday, 10.30 am–5.30 pm.

Awards
1991 & 92   Tea Council Award of Excellence
Egon Ronay recommended

Local Interest:
Falkland Palace, at the centre of the village, was built by James IV in the 16th century. The gardens and tennis court – one of the oldest in Britain – are well worth a visit.

Kind Kyttock was the heroine of a poem by William Dunbar, the early Scots poet. 'The Ballad of Kind Kyttock' tells how she settled in Falkland and served good food and drink to weary travellers. Liz and Bert Dalrymple, who came here from Glasgow 20 years ago to find a more peaceful life, follow her example and offer tasty traditional Scottish fare in a relaxed atmosphere to thousands of visitors every year from all over the world. In fact, a group of Americans arrived one day with a cutting from the *Los Angeles Times* giving a very positive review of Kind Kyttocks, so news of how good it is has obviously spread far and wide.

The menu has an appealing Scottish flavour – Midlothian oatcakes served with cheddar cheese, Scottish pancakes with cream and home-made apricot jam or fresh fruit, traditional Cloutie Dumpling with cream, and an irresistible Rob Roy ice cream with butterscotch sauce and petticoat tail shortbread. All these good things are served in two rooms, upstairs and down, where dark furniture, colourful tablecloths and an interesting selection of prints and paintings on the walls create a very pleasing, old-fashioned atmosphere. *Teas served:* House Blend, Darjeeling, Earl Grey, China, Ceylon, Assam, Russian. *Herbal teas are also offered.*

THE WILLOW TEAROOM

Owner: Anne Mulhern

217 Sauchiehall Street
Glasgow G2 3EX
Tel: 0141 332 0521

Directions
The tearoom is on the first floor above
Henderson the jewellers.

Opening times
Open all year except Sundays.
Monday–Saturday, 9.30 am–4.30 pm.
Sunday, closed.

Award
Egon Ronay recommended

Local Interest:
Within walking distance of the tearoom is the Glasgow
School of Art, the Tenement House (a reconstruction of a
typical Glaswegian tenement block with original domestic
interiors), the Glasgow Concert Hall and the Kelvin Grove
Museum. There are also many other examples of
Mackintosh architecture.

While tea shops often manage to create an impression of past times, the Willow Tearoom is a genuine example of turn-of-the-century design. The Room de Luxe is the only remaining room of Miss Kate Cranston's "tearoom empire", created for her by Charles Rennie Mackintosh in 1904. His wonderful Arts and Crafts style that heralded Art Deco, gave his architecture, furniture, lamps and tableware the strong rectilinear contours and geometric shapes that fascinate the eye. Mackintosh had previously designed the interior for three other Cranston tearooms, but the Willow allowed him to style the exterior and interior of an entire building.

In 1983, the tearoom was restored by the current owner, Anne Mulhern. The mirror friezes, the gesso panel and the ornate leaded doors had happily survived and the chairs and tables were reproduced to Mackintosh's original 1904 design. An unhurried atmosphere matches the elegance of the interior and the comprehensive list of teas, favourite tea-time traditionals and cakes makes this a very special experience. *Teas served:* Tearoom Blend, Breakfast, Earl Grey, Lapsang Souchong, Darjeeling, Ceylon, Assam, Rose Petal, Keemun, Jasmine Blossom, Yunnan, Kenya, Rose Pouchong, Decaffeinated. *Fruit flavoured and herbal teas are also offered.*

THE CHATTERBOX

Owner: Janet Hodge

**73 Victoria Street
Newton Stewart, Wigtownshire
Scotland DG8 6NL
Tel: 01671 403967**

Directions
**Newton Stewart is on the A75 from Dumfries
to Stranraer. Chatterbox is in the main street
near the clock tower, next door to Presto
Supermarket.**

Opening times
Open all year except Sundays.
Monday–Saturday, November–February,
9 am–4.30 pm. Monday–Saturday,
March–October, 9 am–5 pm.
Sunday, closed.

Local Interest:
*Newton Stewart has a small working woollen mill and a
museum documenting the town's history. The area is an
excellent base for visiting the Galloway Forest Park and
the small nearby town of Whithorn.*

Every morning the Chatterbox kitchen is a hive of activity with the team of girls mixing, whisking, kneading and rolling, just to taunt, tease and titillate the taste buds of the stream of customers that turn up for wonderful lunchtime specials and tea-time treats. There are oodles of Scottish dishes on the menu – Galloway Beef, Solway salmon mousse, Hoagie rolls filled with the salad of your choice, Hot Scots Dumplings with cream and custard, Scottish Gingerbread, Border Tart, Dundee Cake, doughnuts (said by one American visitor to be the best between Chatterbox and New York!) and ten dif-

ferent kinds of scone. The menu also advises you to "Good Golly, Look at the Trolley" where you will find wicked favourites such as chocolate nut fudge cake, yogurt cream cake, pavlova, strawberry meringue roulade and many more.

The range of teas, from Brodies of Edinburgh, producers of quality beverages for over 100 years, offers something for everyone, including the rich curranty Connoisseur Blend of Assam, Kenya and Ceylon teas. *Teas served:* House Blend, Darjeeling, Pure China, China-Darjeeling, Assam, Lapsang Souchong, Earl Grey, Ceylon, Keemun.

JEEVES 2000 AND TEAPOT 2000

If you are seeking to brew the perfect pot of tea at home, you will find the two teapots that have been specially designed for The Tea Council will help you achieve your goal. Choose either Jeeves 2000 or Teapot 2000 for easy brewing and stylish serving.

TEAPOT 2000

Specially commissioned by The Tea Council, Teapot 2000 is a completely new way to enjoy tea at just the strength you like, from first cup to last. Beautiful to look at and superbly engineered, it could hardly be simpler to use. With its heatproof handle, clear glass six-cup base, removable filter column, streamlined spout and heat-resistant mat, Teapot 2000 makes tea drinking even more pleasurable than before.

How to use

Lift out the lid and plunger and put the required amount of loose leaf tea into the bottom of the column. Pour on boiling water in the normal way but, to prevent spillage, do not fill beyond 4 cm from the lip of the pot. Replace the lid with the plunger up. When the brew has reached the chosen strength, just push down the plunger to stop further brewing and the tea is ready to pour.

Cleaning and Maintenance

Teapot 2000 should be emptied and cleaned after each use.

To remove column for rinsing, simply turn (when cool) until one of the side lugs is lined up with the spout, then lift out. To replace the column in the pot, fit one of the side lugs into the spout and turn the column until securely fixed.

All parts should be cleaned after use with hot water and detergent. All parts can be washed in a dishwasher using the normal cycle.

Spare Parts

The following parts are available separately: brewing column (i.e. filter, lid and plunger); glass base; cork mat.

TEAPOT 2000 £19.50

plus £3.00 postage and packing

For more information or to order your Teapot 2000 Teapot please telephone

0181 398 9174 (24 hours)

or write to
The Tea Council, PO Box 9B
East Molesey, Surrey KT8 0PE

You can place your order by Access or Visa. Please allow 28 days delivery (UK mainland only). *14 day money back guarantee.*

JEEVES 2000 TEAPOT

Jeeves 2000 has been exclusively commissioned by The Tea Council to bring you the latest way to enjoy tea at just the strength you like, from first cup to last. It is a classic English pot design crafted to the highest quality.

HOW TO USE

With its earthenware six-cup base and removable filter column, Jeeves 2000 is a real pleasure to use. Lift out the lid and put the required amount of loose leaf tea into the bottom of the column. Pour on boiling water in the normal way. Replace the lid with the plunger up. When the brew has reached the chosen strength, just push down the plunger to stop further brewing and the tea is ready to pour.

CLEANING AND MAINTENANCE

Jeeves 2000 should be emptied and rinsed after each use.

To remove the column for rinsing, simply turn it (when cool) until one of the side lugs is in the notch on the rim, then lift out. To replace the column, fit one of the side lugs back into the notch on the rim and turn the column until it is securely fixed.

All parts should be cleaned after use with hot water and detergent. All parts can be washed in a dishwasher using the normal wash cycle.

SPARE PARTS

The following parts are available separately: brewing column (i.e. filter and plunger); earthenware base.

JEEVES 2000 £19.50
plus £3.00 postage and packing

For more information or to order your Jeeves 2000 Teapot please telephone

0181 398 9174 (24 hours)

or write to
The Tea Council, PO Box 9B
East Molesey, Surrey KT8 0PE

You can place your order by Access or Visa.
Please allow 28 days delivery (UK mainland only).
14 day money back guarantee.

LEADING UK TEA SUPPLIERS

UK Blenders & Packers
Accord Services Ltd
Ahmad Tea Ltd
Barber Kingsmark
Big T (Tea) Ltd
   Ismail & Co Ltd
Brodie Melrose Drysdale & Co
Char Wallahs Ltd
Chase Tea & Coffee Co
Chelsea Foods Ltd
D J Miles & Co
Gala Coffee & Tea Ltd
George Payne & Co Ltd
Hankow Batchelor Tea Co Ltd
Horne & Sutton Ltd
Imporient Tea & Coffee Ltd
Jacksons Foods Ltd
Kamet Ltd
Keith Spicer Ltd
Langdons (Coffee & Tea) Ltd
Matthew Algie & Co Ltd
Nairobi Coffee & Tea Ltd

New English Teas Ltd
Norfolk Tea & Coffee
Northern Tea Merchants
Premier Beverages
   Glengettie Tea Co Ltd
   London Herb & Spice Co Ltd
   Melrose Ltd
   Ridgways
Regency Tea Co Ltd
Ringtons Ltd
   Samuel Kaye & Son Ltd
R Twining & Co Ltd
   Jackson of Piccadilly Ltd
   Namosa Ltd
Taylors Tea & Coffee Ltd
Tetley GB Ltd
Tudor Tea & Coffee
Unilever Export Ltd
Van den Bergh Food Services
Whittard of Chelsea
Williamson & Magor Ltd
Windmill Tea Company

INDEX OF TEA SHOPS

GENERAL INDEX